Edward Gordon Duff

The Printers, Stationers and Bookbinders of London and Westminster in the Fifteenth Century

Edward Gordon Duff

The Printers, Stationers and Bookbinders of London and Westminster in the Fifteenth Century

ISBN/EAN: 9783337249755

Printed in Europe, USA, Canada, Australia, Japan

Cover: Foto ©ninafisch / pixelio.de

More available books at **www.hansebooks.com**

The Printers, Stationers and Bookbinders of London and Westminster in the Fifteenth Century

By

E. Gordon Duff, M.A. Oxon.

Sandars Reader in Bibliography in the
University of Cambridge, 1898-1899

Privately Printed
1899

THE SANDARS LECTURES

1898-1899

ABERDEEN UNIVERSITY PRESS

THE PRINTERS, STATIONERS AND BOOKBINDERS OF LONDON AND WESTMINSTER IN THE FIFTEENTH CENTURY. A SERIES OF FOUR LECTURES DELIVERED AT CAMBRIDGE IN THE LENT TERM, MDCCCIC.

BY

E. GORDON DUFF, M.A. Oxon.

SANDARS READER IN BIBLIOGRAPHY IN THE
UNIVERSITY OF CAMBRIDGE, 1898-1899

PRIVATELY PRINTED
1899

EDÉSKI EDÉSTAR.

Ai, Pirinó! t'astís te 'mē stārás
Akáva tem te bānges Yov kērdás
　Nai kotoréndi pagerásas les
Te fetedér ta vaver tem kērás?

CONTENTS.

LECTURE I.
The Printers at Westminster

LECTURE II.
The Printers at London

LECTURE III.
The Stationers

LECTURE IV.
The Bookbinders

LECTURE I.

THE PRINTERS AT WESTMINSTER.

WHILE the history of the invention and introduction of the art of printing into the various countries of Europe is not only obscure, but still the subject of endless controversy, the history of its introduction into England is now practically settled.

There are no troublesome and incomprehensible documents as in the case of France. No questionable references or undatable fragments such as Dutch and German bibliographers have to contend with. The only attempt that has been made to bring forward an earlier printer than William Caxton is founded upon the misprinted date in the first book printed at Oxford.

In 1664, while the Company of Stationers and the King were quarrelling over the question of which had or should have the most power in matters pertaining to printing, a certain Richard Atkyns put forth a tract, now exceedingly rare, called *The Original and Growth of Printing*. In this tract, intended to uphold the king's rights, attention was drawn for the first time to the Oxford book. "A book came into my hands" writes Atkyns, "printed at Oxford, A.D. 1468, which was three years before any of the recited authors would allow it to be in England." Around this book Atkyns wove a wonderful romance, in the style of the earlier legends about Coster and Gutenberg. Rumours of the new art, he suggests, having reached England, trusted men were sent over to bribe or kidnap an eligible printer and bring him over secretly, along with a press, type and other impedimenta, to England. This was accordingly done, and a certain Frederick Corsellis was conveyed into England, and set up a press in Oxford. One curious point has escaped all commentators on this story, and that is that a real person named Corsellis did come over to England from the Low Countries about that time, and was an ancestor of several well-known London families in Atkyns' time, such as the Van Ackers, the Wittewronges and the Middletons.

Atkyns referred for evidence to documents which have never been found, and his story has met with the disbelief it deserved, but the Oxford book with the date of 1468 not only exists, but has still supporters who consider, or say they consider, the date to be genuine.

Singer in the early part of the century wrote a book in favour of its authenticity, though, as he afterwards attempted to suppress his work, we may conclude he had changed his opinion. Mr Madan of the Bodleian, in his recent admirable history of Oxford printing, clings hesitatingly to 1468, "but quaere" as he would himself say. Generally, however, it is agreed that the date is a misprint for 1478. The book has signatures which are not known to have been used before 1472, and when the book is placed alongside the two others, issued from the same press in 1479 and printed in the same type, it falls naturally into its proper place, taking just the small precedence which its slightly lesser excellence of workmanship warrants.

Having now disposed of Caxton's only rival, let us turn to Caxton himself. It would, I think, be out of place here, to recapitulate however shortly the history of Caxton's early life, since it has been so fully and excellently done in that standard book, familiar to you all, Blades's *Life of Caxton*. What is more to our purpose is to pass on to the time when, as an influential and prosperous man, he laid the foundations of his career as a printer. By 1463 Caxton had been appointed to the office of governor of the English nation in the Low Countries, a post of considerable importance, and entailing the supervision of trade and traders, and this office he held until about the year 1469. At this latter date he was also in the service of the Duchess of Burgundy, though in what capacity is not stated, but he certainly employed himself at her request in making translations of romances. The *Recuyell of the Histories of Troye*, a well-known romance of the period, was translated between the years 1469 and 1471, and presented to the duchess in September of the latter year. In the prologue of the printed edition Caxton explains that after the duchess had received her copy, many other persons desired copies also, but that finding the labour of writing too wearisome for him, and not expeditious enough for his friends, he had "practised and learnt, at his great charge and expense, to ordain the book in print, to the end that every man might have them at once".

Now in 1471, when Caxton finished his translation of the *Recueil*, he was living at Cologne, a city remarkable even at that time for the number of its printers, and the first town that Caxton had visited where the art was practised. He had just finished the tedious copying of a large MS., so that the advantages of printing would be manifest to him, and we may be tolerably certain that it was about this time and at this town that he took his first lessons in the art and mastered the mechanical processes.

Printing by this time had ceased to be a secret art, nor was there such a demand for books as to make it a very valuable one. The printed books of Germany had at an early date found their way to Bruges, and people's eyes were accustomed to the sight of the printed page, though the nobles still preferred MSS., as being more ornamental and costly. There are copies in the Cambridge University Library and at Lambeth of the *Cicero de officiis*, printed at Mainz by Schoiffer in 1466, which were bought in 1467 at

Bruges by John Russell, afterwards Bishop of Lincoln, when abroad on a diplomatic mission; and a speech of his, delivered at Ghent in 1470, on the occasion of the investiture of the Duke of Burgundy with the order of the Garter, was one of Caxton's earliest printed productions.

A very strong piece of evidence to my mind that Caxton learnt at Cologne is to be found in the prologue to the English translation of the *De proprietatibus rerum*, by Bartholomæus Anglicus, which was printed by W. de Worde, Caxton's apprentice and successor, in 1496. This prologue, written by De Worde himself, contains these lines:—

> And also of your charyte call to remembraunce,
>   The soule of William Caxton, the fyrste prynter of this book,
> In Laten tongue at Coleyn, hymself to avaunce,
>   That every well disposed man, may thereon look.

Now this is a perfectly clear statement that Caxton printed a *Bartholomæus* in Latin at Cologne, and we know an edition of the book manifestly printed at Cologne about the time Caxton was there. The type in which it is printed greatly resembles that of some other Cologne printers, and it seems to be connected with some of Caxton's Bruges types. At any rate, the story cannot be put aside as without foundation. It is not, of course, suggested that Caxton printed the book by himself or owned the materials, but only that he assisted in its production. He was learning the art of printing in the office where this book was being prepared, and his practical knowledge was acquired by assisting to print it.

Returning to Bruges, he set about turning his knowledge to account, and in partnership with a writer of manuscripts, named Colard Mansion, began to make or obtain the necessary materials.

About 1475 their first book was issued, the *Recuyell of the Histories of Troye*, the first book printed in the English language. It is a small thick folio of 352 leaves, and though not uncommon in an imperfect condition, is of the very greatest rarity when perfect. Two other books were printed before 1477, *The Game and Play of the Chess* and the *Quatre derrenières choses*, the latter a very rare book, of which only two copies are known.

In 1477 the Duke of Burgundy was killed, and the duchess had to resign her position and retire into comparative privacy. Caxton's employment was at an end, and his services no longer required at the court. It was, probably, for this reason that his thoughts turned to his native land. He dissolved his partnership with Colard Mansion, and taking with him some of the printing material set out for England.

It must have been early in 1477 that Caxton returned and set to work. He took up his residence in Westminster at a house with the heraldic sign of the "Red Pale," which was situated in the Almonry, a place close to the Abbey where alms were distributed to the poor, and where Margaret, Countess of Richmond, the mother of Henry VII., and a great patroness of learning, built alms-houses. The exact position of Caxton's house is not known, but it was probably on some part of the ground now covered by the Westminster Aquarium.

The first book printed in England was the *Dictes or sayengis of the Philosophers*, translated from the French by Earl Rivers, a friend and patron of Caxton, and edited by Caxton himself, who added the chapter "concernyng wymmen," a chapter which, with its prologue, exhibits a considerable amount of humour.

It is interesting to notice that, as the book is in English, we alone of European nations started our press with a book in the vernacular.

The ordinary copies of the *Dictes* are without colophon, though the printer and year are in the epilogue, but a copy formerly in the Althorp Library and now at Manchester has an imprint which states that the book was finished on the 18th November, 1477. Although we count the *Dictes or Sayengis* as the first book printed in England on account of its being the first dated book, it is quite possible that some may have preceded it. Between the time of Caxton's arrival in 1477 and the end of 1478 about twenty-one books were printed, and only two have imprints, so that the rest are merely ranged conjecturally by the evidence of type or other details. Now in 1510 W. de Worde issued an edition of *King Apolyn of Tyre*, translated from the French by one of his assistants, Robert Copland, who in his preface writes as follows: "My worshipful master Wynken de Worde, having a little book of an ancient history of a kyng, sometyme reigning in the countree of Thyre called Appolyn, concernynge his malfortunes and peryllous aduentures right espouuentables, bryefly compyled and pyteous for to here, the which boke I Robert Coplande have me applyed for to translate out of the Frensshe language into our maternal Englysshe tongue at the exhortacion of my forsayd mayster, accordynge dyrectly to myn auctor, gladly followynge the trace of my mayster Caxton, begynnynge with small storyes and pamfletes and so to other". Now this Robert Copland was spoken of a little later as the oldest printer in England, so that he may well have known a good deal about the beginning of Caxton's career. We find a very similar case in Scotland. Printing was introduced there mainly for the purpose of printing the Aberdeen Breviary, but the first thing the printers did was to issue a series of small poetical pieces by Dunbar, Chaucer and others, an exactly similar kind of set to the small Caxton pieces in the Cambridge University Library.

In connexion with these Caxton pieces I noticed the other day a strange statement. The writer was speaking of Henry Bradshaw's knowledge of Caxton, and went on to say that "to his bibliographical genius the Cambridge University Library owes the possession of its many unique Caxtons and unique Caxton fragments". The library, however, owes them mainly to the much-maligned John Bagford, who collected the early English books which came to the university with Bishop More's library. The monstrous collection of title-pages in the British Museum, generally associated with Bagford's name, was made by the venerated founder of English bibliography, Joseph Ames.

Before the end of 1478 Caxton had printed about twenty-one books. Of these sixteen were small works all containing less than fifty leaves; of the others the most important is the first edition of the *Canterbury Tales*, of which there is, I think, no perfect copy. Blades speaks of a fine perfect copy in the library of Merton College, Oxford, and remarks also that Dibdin ignorantly spoke of it as imperfect. In Dibdin's time, however, it certainly was imperfect, for I have seen some notes of Lord Spencer's referring to his having sent some leaves from an imperfect copy to the college to assist them in perfecting their own.

Among the other books of the period of special interest is the *Propositio Johannis Russell*, which has often been ascribed to the Bruges press, as the speech of which it consists was delivered in the Low Countries. Lord Spencer's copy had a curious history. It is bound up in a volume of English and Latin MS., and in the Brand sale in 1807 the volume appeared among the MSS., with a note, "A work on Theology and Religion, with five leaves at the end, a very great curiosity, very early printed on wooden blocks or type". It was bought by the Marquis of Blandford for forty-five shillings, and at his sale ten years after cost Lord Spencer £126.

Another interesting book is the *Infancia Salvatoris*, of which the only known copy is at Göttingen, being one of the two unique Caxtons which are in foreign libraries. It was originally in the Harleian Library, which was sold entire to Osborne the bookseller, and was bought with many other books for the Göttingen University. It is in its old red Harleian binding, with Osborne's price, fifteen shillings marked inside, and the note of the Göttingen librarian: "aus dem Katalogen Thomas Osborne in London 12 Maii 1749 (No. 4179) erkauft".

In the first group of books comes also the only printed edition of the *Sarum Ordinale* or *Pica*, which was superseded by Clement Maydeston's *Directorium Sacerdotum*. Unfortunately the book is only known from some fragments rescued from a binding and now in the British Museum. To it refers the curious little advertisement put out by Caxton, the only example of a printer's advertisement in England in the fifteenth century, though we know of many foreign specimens: "If it plese ony man spirituel or temporel to bye ony pyes of two and thre comemoracions of salisburi use, enpryntid after the forme of this present lettre whiche ben wel and truly correct late hym come to westmonester in to the almonesrye at the reed pale and he shal haue them good chepe". So far the advertisement; below it is the appeal to the public, "Supplico stet cedula". It seems curious that this should be in Latin, for one would naturally suppose that the ones most likely to tear down the advertisement would be the persons ignorant of that language.

Two copies of this advertisement are known, one in the Bodleian, and another, formerly in the Althorp collection, at Manchester. It has been suggested that both copies may have been at one time extracted from some old binding in the Cambridge University Library. The example at Manchester certainly belonged at one time to Richard Farmer, who was University librarian, but the Bodleian example was found by Francis Douce in a binding in his own collection.

The group of eight small books in the University Library which I spoke of as perhaps printed earlier than the *Dictes or Sayengis* were originally all bound together in one volume in old calf, and lettered " Old poetry printed by Caxton". This precious volume contained the *Stans Puer ad Mensam*, the *Parvus Catho*, *The Chorle and the Bird*, *The Horse the Shepe and the Goose*, *The Temple of Glas*, *The Temple of Brass*, *The Book of Courtesy* and *Anelida and Arcyte*, and of five of these no other copies are known.

About 1478-9 was issued the *Rhetorica Nova* of Laurentius of Savona, of which two copies are known, one in the library of Corpus Christi College, Cambridge, the other in the University Library of Upsala. Now although this book had been known and examined by many for two hundred years, and is printed in the most widely used of Caxton's types, yet it was not recognised as a Caxton until it was examined by Henry Bradshaw in 1861. The colophon says that the work was compiled in the University of Cambridge in 1478, and it was in consequence described by all the early writers as the first book printed at Cambridge. Strype wrote an account of the Corpus copy to Bagford, who in his turn wrote of it to Tanner, and he in his turn communicated it to Ames. Ames then inserted it at the head of his list of books printed at Cambridge, and the mistake, as is usual in such cases, was copied in turn by each succeeding writer on printing.

In 1480 considerable changes are to be found in Caxton's methods of work, owing no doubt to competition, for in this year a press was started in London by a certain John Lettou. He appears to have been a practised printer, and his work is certainly better than Caxton's, his type much smaller and neater, and the page more regularly printed. He also introduced into England the use of signatures. Signatures are the small letters printed at the foot of the page which were intended to serve as a guide to the bookbinder in gathering up the sheets in their right order. From the earliest times they were put in in writing both in MSS. and the earliest printed books, but about 1472 printers began to print them in in type, and the habit soon became general. Caxton's use of signatures begins in 1480, and was doubtless copied from the London printer.

At the beginning of 1480 Caxton had printed an indulgence in his large type, the second of his founts, and immediately afterwards the London printer issued another edition in his small neat type. Caxton promptly had another fount cut of small type, and issued with it a third edition of the indulgence.

It is a matter much to be regretted that Henry Bradshaw never issued one of his *Memoranda* on the subject of these indulgences, for he had collected much interesting information, and was the first to point out the variations in the wording of the different issues as well as the discoverer of several unknown examples.

The year 1480 also saw the introduction of illustrations, which were first used in the *Mirror of the World*. In it there are two sets of cuts, one depicting various masters, either alone or with several pupils, the other are merely diagrams copied from those found in MSS. of the work. These diagrams are meagre and difficult to understand, so much so that the printer himself has put several in their wrong places. The explanatory words inside the diagrams, which would no doubt have been printed in type had Caxton had a fount small enough, are written by hand. It is interesting to notice that in all copies of the book the same handwriting is found, though I am afraid it would be unsafe to conclude it to be Caxton's. The period from 1480 to 1483 is the least interesting as regards Caxton's books. Besides the *Mirror of the World* only two books contain woodcuts; the *Catho*, and the second edition of the *Game and Play of the Chess*. The two cuts in the *Catho* had been used before in the *Mirror*, but the sixteen in the chess-book are specially cut, though clearly by a different artist from the one who made those for the *Mirror*. Mr Linton in his book on wood-engraving expressed the opinion that many of these cuts were of soft metal, treated in the same manner as a wood-block, but whenever we find any of them in use for a long period, the breaks which occur in them and the occurrence sometimes even of worm holes show that the cut must have been of wood.

Among the other books of this period are the first and second editions of *Caxton's Chronicle*, and *Higden's Polycronicon*. The unique copy of the Latin *Psalter* in the British Museum, a Caxton which remained unidentified until fairly recently, also belongs to about 1480, but perhaps the most interesting book of all is the first edition in English of *Reynard the Fox*. This was translated by Caxton from the Dutch, the translation being finished in June, 1481, and the book evidently printed at once. It is curious that this book which would lend itself so readily to illustration was not printed with woodcuts, but Caxton after using them in 1480 made no further move in this direction until 1484, when another group of illustrated books appeared. It always looks as though Caxton, and indeed his own words tend to prove it, was much more interested in the literary side of his work than in the mechanical, and therefore only called in the aid of the wood-engraver when he thought it absolutely necessary. He wished his books to be purchased on their merits alone, and therefore did not try, like the later printers, to use illustrations merely to attract the unwary purchaser. On the other hand, as none of the other printers in England issued illustrated books, he had no competition to contend with.

A book which may have been printed about this time, but if so has entirely disappeared, is a translation of the *Metamorphoses of Ovid*. In the Pepysian Library is a MS.

of books x.-xv., with the following colophon: "Translated and fynysshed by me William Caxton at Westmestre, the 22 day of Apryll, the yere of our lord 1480 And the 20 yere of the Regne of kyng Edward the fourth". It seems very improbable Caxton would have taken the trouble to make this translation had he not intended it to be printed, and he mentions it in one of his prologues amongst a series of books which he had translated and printed. This MS. was bought by Pepys at an auction in 1688.

The period from 1483 to 1486 is more interesting. First in order comes the first edition of Mirk's *Liber festivalis* and its supplement the *Quattuor sermones*. The next is a small quarto pamphlet known as the *Sex quam elegantissimæ epistolæ*, and consisting of letters that passed between Sixtus IV. and the Venetian Republic. The only copy known was found bound up in a volume of seventeenth century theological tracts in the library at Halberstadt, and was sold in 1890 to the British Museum for £200. After these come a series of English writers, Lidgate's *Life of Our Lady*; Chaucer's *Canterbury Tales*, *Troilus and Cressida*, and *Hous of Fame*; Gower's *Confessio amantis*, and the *Life of St. Wenefrede*. The *Canterbury Tales* is the second edition published by Caxton, and has a peculiarly interesting preface by the printer, in which he tells us that having some six years before printed the *Canterbury Tales*, which were sold to many and divers gentlemen, one of the number had complained that the text was corrupt. He said, however, that his father had a very fine MS. of the poem which he valued highly, but that he thought he might be able to borrow it. Caxton at once promised that if this could be done, he would reprint the book. This second edition is ornamented with a series of cuts of the different characters, and one of all the pilgrims seated together at supper at an immense round table. This cut does duty several times later on as the frontispiece to Lidgate's *Assembly of the Gods*.

In the same year as the *Canterbury Tales*, appeared two other illustrated books, the *Fables of Esop*, and the *Golden Legend*. The *Esop* has one large full-page cut of Esop used as a frontispiece and which is found only in the Queen's copy at Windsor, and no less than a hundred and eighty-five smaller cuts, the work of two if not three engravers, one being evidently the man who made the cuts for the chess-book.

The *Golden Legend* is the largest book ever printed by Caxton. It contains 449 leaves, and is printed on a much larger-sized paper than he ever used elsewhere, the full sheet measuring about two feet by sixteen inches. The frontispiece is a large woodcut representing the saints in glory, while in addition there are eighteen large and fifty-two small cuts, the large series including one of the device of the Earl of Arundel, to whom the book is dedicated. The three dated books of 1485 are all especially important. The first is the first edition of the *Morte d' Arthur*, surely the most covetable of all Caxton's books. For many years only one copy was known in the library of Osterley Park, and many were the attempts made by the two great Caxton collectors in the early years of the century, Lord Spencer and his nephew, the Duke of Devonshire, to obtain the treasure. The Duke of Devonshire almost succeeded, but was foiled by some awkward clause in a deed. However, another copy appeared at a sale in Wales, wanting four leaves, but otherwise in beautiful condition, and this was bought by Lord Spencer. The Osterley Park copy was sold in 1885 for £1950, and went to America, and after several changes of ownership now belongs, I believe, to Mr. Hoe of New York. The other two dated books are the *Life of thate Noble and Christian Prince, Charles the Great*, and the *History of the Knight Paris and Fair Vienne*. Both of these books were translated by Caxton from the French. Only one copy of each is known, and both are in the British Museum.

After 1485 Caxton's energy began to decline, or at any rate we know of fewer books having been issued during the period from 1486 to 1489. The *Speculum vitæ Christi* and the *Royal Book* belong to 1486, and are illustrated with woodcuts of a very much superior execution to those which had been previously in use; they are not large but are simply and gracefully designed. Besides the regular series in the *Speculum* specially cut for it, a few very small and rather roughly designed cuts are found, evidently cut for use in one of the editions of the Sarum *Horæ*, which were issued at an earlier date, but of which nothing now remains but a few odd leaves. It is interesting to notice that in neither edition of the *Speculum* which he printed did Caxton use the full series of the cuts which had been engraved for it; for several years afterwards one or two cuts occur in books printed by Caxton's successor, evidently part of the series, and which he had never used himself. To this time may be ascribed the newest Caxton discovery, two fragments printed on vellum of an edition of the *Donatus Melior*, revised by Mancinellus, which were discovered some few years ago by Mr. Proctor in the binding of a book in the library of New College, Oxford.

In 1487 Caxton was anxious to issue an edition of the Sarum *Missal*, and, not considering his own type suitable for the purpose, commissioned a Paris printer named William Maynyal to print one for him. Who this Paris printer was is a matter of mystery, for his name is found in no other book, but he was perhaps a relative of a certain George Maynyal who printed at Paris about 1480. The *Missal* is a very handsome book, printed in red and black, and with two fine woodcuts at the Canon. The only known copy, which belongs to Lord Newton of Lyme Park, appears to have met at an early date with bad treatment, and wants some seventeen leaves, mostly at the beginning.

In this book for the first time Caxton used his well-known

device, consisting of his trade or merchant's mark, with his initials on either side.

Whether this device was cut in England or abroad has long been a vexed question, but as it has no resemblance to any foreign device of the period, and as the execution is poor and coarse, we may conclude safely that it is of native work. Caxton, no doubt, wished to call attention to the fact, which might have escaped notice, that the book was produced for him and at his cost; and so when the copies of the book had been delivered to him at Westminster he had the device cut, and stamped it on the last leaf of each copy. In this edition the portion of the marriage service in English has been omitted by the printer, who has left blank spaces for it to be filled in with the pen. There was an edition of the Sarum *Legenda* issued about the same time, which is known now only from a few odd leaves rescued from book-bindings. It agrees in every way typographically with the *Missal*, it is in the same type, has the same number of lines to the page, every detail the same, so I think we have good reason for supposing that it also was printed by Maynyal for Caxton. Bradshaw suggested Higman, the Paris printer, as the printer of these fragments, so that Maynyal may have had some business connexion with him.

The second edition of the *Golden Legend* came out shortly after this, that is about 1488, and is a difficult book to explain typographically. About 200 leaves are of the first edition, while the beginning, a small piece of the middle, and the end are of the second. Now it is curious that no copy in existence seems to be correctly made up as one edition or the other, and the most probable explanation seems to be that part of the stock happening to get damaged, a reprint was made to complete what was left, and that sheets were picked indiscriminately. The most nearly perfect second issue that I have seen is the one at Aberdeen, but it is imperfect at beginning and end. The copy in the

Hunterian Museum at Glasgow has a second edition ending, but I have not yet been able to discover a copy with a second edition beginning.

In 1489 two editions of an indulgence from Joannes de Gigliis were issued, printed in a type used nowhere else by Caxton and not mentioned by Blades. The earliest noticed of these indulgences was discovered in the following manner. Cotton, who found it at Dublin, published an account of it in the second part of his *Typographical Gazetteer* in 1862, and he there described it as a product of the early Oxford press. Bradshaw obtained a photograph of it, and at once conjectured from the form and appearance of the type that it was printed by Caxton. He immediately communicated his discovery to Blades, who, however, refused to accept it as a product of Caxton's press without further proof, and it was never mentioned in any edition of his books on that printer. The necessary proof was soon afterwards forthcoming, for Bradshaw found that in a book printed by W. de Worde in 1494, the sidenotes were in this identical type, and as De Worde was the inheritor of all Caxton's material, this fount must have belonged to him.

About the same year were issued two unique books, *The History of Blanchardin and Eglantine*, and the *Four Sons of Aymon*.

The *Blanchardin* is unfortunately imperfect, wanting all the end, and it is impossible to say of how much this consists. The *Four Sons of Aymon* is also imperfect, wanting a few leaves at the beginning. Both books were formerly in the Spencer Library. The *Doctrinal of Sapience* published in 1489 is a translation by Caxton from a French version, and one particular copy of it in the Queen's library at Windsor is worthy of special notice. It is printed throughout upon vellum, a material which Caxton hardly ever used, the only other complete book so printed being a copy of the *Speculum vitæ Christi* in the British Museum.

This particular copy of the *Doctrinal* has also a special chapter added " Of the negligences happyng in the masse and of the remedyes " which is not found in any other copy. That it was specially printed is evident from its concluding words, " This chapitre to fore I durst not sette in the boke by cause it is not conuenyent ne aparteynyng that euery layman sholde knowe it ".

During the last year or two of his life most of the books issued by Caxton were of a religious nature. Some would have us believe that this was owing to illness or a premonition of his own approaching end, some to the fact that his wife, if the Maud Caxton who was buried in 1490 was his wife, was just dead. Both these ideas seem to me rather fanciful. He no doubt printed what was most in demand. One book issued about this time was certainly not religious. It is a free paraphrase of some portions of the *Æneid* and was translated by Caxton from the French. It does not pretend to be a translation of the original, but was abused soundly by Gavin Douglas, who issued a translation in 1553, for its many inaccuracies. Amongst the religious books I may mention the *Ars Moriendi*, a little quarto of eight leaves, which was discovered by Henry Bradshaw in a volume of tracts in the Bodleian, and of which no other copy is known, and the very interesting *Commemoratio lamentationis beate Marie*, which is in the University Library at Ghent and which is one of the two unique Caxtons on the continent. It was I believe picked up by one of the librarians bound in a volume of tracts and by him presented to the University Library. This Caxton picked off a stall in Belgium may be considered as the real successor to the imaginary one picked off the stall in Holland by the celebrated Snuffy Davy of the *Antiquary*.

The *Fifteen Oes* is another of these religious books. Its name is taken from the fact that each of the fifteen prayers of which it is composed begins with O, and it was printed as a supplement to a Sarum *Horæ*, with later editions of which it was generally incorporated. It contains a beautiful woodcut of the Crucifixion, and is also the only existing book printed by Caxton which had borders round the pages. That a *Horæ* to accompany it was printed is most probable, for the Crucifixion is only one of a set of cuts which was used, together with the borders, in an edition printed about 1494.

Though most of the books at this time can only be arranged conjecturally, it is probable that the last book printed by Caxton was the *Book of Divers Ghostly Matters*. It consists really of three tracts, each separately printed, the *Seven Points of True Love*, the *Twelve Profits of Tribulation*, and the *Rule of St. Benet;* but as they are always found bound together, they are classed as one book. There is one cut in the second treatise taken from the *Speculum* series, but no other illustrations.

Caxton used during his career eight founts of type, of which six only are included in Blades's enumeration. The late French type which appeared about 1490-91, and is found in a few of the latest books, such as the *Ars Moriendi* and the *Fifteen Oes*, Blades considered not to have been used until after Caxton's death; and the type of the 1489 indulgences was not mentioned at all. Blades's arrangement, too, of the books under their types, though correct in a certain way, is a very misleading one, for he takes the types in their order, and then arranges all the books under the type in which the body of the book is printed. Now this leads to considerable confusion when different types were in use together. For instance, Caxton started at Westminster with types 2 and 3, and both are used in his first book, but Blades puts the books in type 3 after all those in type 2, and thus the Sarum *Ordinale*, perhaps the second book printed in England, certainly one of the earliest, comes thirty-sixth on his list. Now, though Blades's arrangement was not a chronological one, most writers have made the mistake of thinking so, and have followed it as such, as may be seen, for instance, in the list appended to Caxton's life in the *Dictionary of National Biography*, which follows Blades's arrangement, without any reference to his system or mention of the types.

Caxton printed in England ninety-eight separate books, and, counting in the three printed by him at Bruges, altogether a hundred and one, of which ninety-four are mentioned by Blades. It is true that Blades describes ninety-nine books, but he includes two certainly printed at Bruges after Caxton had left and three printed by De Worde after Caxton's death. But it is not the mere number of the books he printed that makes Caxton's career so remarkable, but the fact that he edited almost every book he issued, and translated a large number. He himself says that he had translated twenty-two, and the statement was made at a time previous to his making several others, and when we consider that amongst his translations is to be included such a large book as the *Golden Legend*, we can only wonder that he printed as much as he did.

Of the exact date of his death we have no evidence, but it evidently must have taken place in 1491. It is unfortunate, too, that no copy of his will has been preserved, though it is quite probable that it may yet be found among the immense mass of documents belonging to Westminster Abbey, and which are now in process of examination. The will, besides the interesting personal details which it might supply, would most likely give some information about those engaged with him in business, the assistants who worked his presses, or the stationers who sold his books.

Of his family we know next to nothing. We know that he was married and had a daughter named Elizabeth, who was married to a merchant named Gerard Croppe, from whom she obtained a deed of separation in 1496. Had Caxton had a son he would probably have continued the printing business. As it was his printing materials were inherited by his assistant or apprentice, Wynkyn de Worde, who continued to carry on work in his old master's house at Westminster. In his letters of denization, taken out so late as the 20th April, 1496, he is described as a printer, and a native of the Duchy of Lorraine. His name, De Worde, which some have fallen into the mistake of deriving from the town of Woerden in Holland, is clearly taken from the town of Worth in Alsace; indeed, the printer sometimes uses the form Worth in place of Worde. Although he inherited Caxton's business, which was, no doubt a flourishing one, he seems to have started on his own account with very little vigour or enterprise. Indeed, so torpid was the press at that time that foreign printers found it worth their while to produce and import reprints of Caxton's books for sale in this country, books to which I shall refer more fully in a future lecture. We soon see that we have to deal now with a man who was merely a mechanic, and who was quite unable to fill the place of Caxton either as an editor or a translator, one who preferred to issue small popular books of a kind to attract the general public, rather than the class of book which had hitherto been published from Caxton's house.

For the first two years De Worde contented himself with using Caxton's old types, of which he appears to have possessed at least five founts, and in that time he printed five books, the *Book of Courtesy*, the *Treatise of Love*, the *Chastising of God's Children*, the *Life of St. Katherine*, and a third edition of the *Golden Legend*. Why this book should have been so often printed is rather a mystery, for, while Caxton issued two editions and De Worde another two before 1500, at the end of the century a considerable number of Caxton's edition still remained for sale at the price of thirteen shillings and fourpence, not a large sum for those days and considering the size of the book.

The *Book of Courtesy*, which is known only from a proof

of two leaves, in the Douce collection at Oxford, was a reprint from Caxton's edition, of which the only known copy is in the Cambridge University Library. In the proof leaves in the Bodleian, De Worde's device is printed upside-down, and for this reason, perhaps, the proof was rejected and used to line a binding, and thus preserved for us. The *Treatise of Love* was printed for the translator, whose name, unfortunately does not appear, but the translation is dated 1493, and the printing is clearly of the same year. The *Chastising of God's Children*, a deplorably dull book, is interesting typographically as being the first book printed at Westminster with a title-page. Why Caxton never introduced this improvement it is hard to say, for he must have seen many books in which they were used, and a book with one was printed at London before his death.

The imprint of the *Golden Legend* is curious, for though it is dated 1493 it contains Caxton's name. De Worde seems to have reprinted from an earlier edition, merely altering the date, or perhaps he meant the words "By me William Caxton" to refer to the translator rather than the printer.

In 1493, very nearly at the close of the year, De Worde's first type makes its appearance in an edition of the *Liber Festivalis*, the second or companion part of the book, the *Quattuor Sermones* coming out early in 1494. The type has a strong French appearance, though it retains several characteristics and even a few identical letters of Caxton's founts. It is curious that up to this time De Worde had not put his name to any book, though most of them contain his first device, a copy on a small scale of Caxton's, and evidently cut in metal.

In 1494 two important books were issued, the *Scala perfeccionis* of Walter Hylton, a Carthusian monk, and a reprint of the *Speculum vite Christi*, both being in the late French type of Caxton. The *Scala perfeccionis* is a rare book when it contains the last part, which is only found in two or three copies. It has on the title-page a woodcut of the Virgin and Child under a canopy, and below this the sentence beginning " Sit dulce nomen domini nostri Jesu Christi benedictum," but the engraver in cutting the block has not attempted to cut the words properly, but merely to give their general appearance, so that the result though decorative is almost impossible to decipher.

The *Speculum* of this year has many points of interest, the chief perhaps being that Caxton's small type No. 7 is found in it, the only time it is used in a printed book, though it had been used before in 1489 for printing indulgences. The text of the book is in Caxton's French type, but the sidenotes are in this small Caxton type up to about the middle of the book, whence the notes are continued in the same type as the text. Up till a year or two ago only one copy of this book was known in Lord Leicester's library at Holkam, but lately another copy, imperfect and in bad condition, turned up amongst some rubbish in the offices of a solicitor at Birkenhead. Three editions of the *Horae ad usum Sarum*, two in quarto and one in octavo, printed in the same type as the other two books, may also be ascribed to 1494. The two in quarto are evidently reprinted from the last edition of Caxton's of which the little treatise called the *Fifteen Oes* formed part, for they have the same borders, and the woodcuts are clearly of sets which belonged to Caxton. The octavo edition is quite different, having no borders, and the woodcuts so far as is known, for the book is only known from a fragment, belong to a set which do not appear to have been used again.

The most famous of the cuts used at this time is one of the Crucifixion (the one used by Caxton in the *Fifteen Oes*), of which a facsimile is given by Dibdin on page 79, volume 2, of his *Typographical Antiquities*. He erroneously remarks about it in another place, "The woodcut of the Crucifixion was never introduced by Caxton, it is too spirited and elegant to harmonise with anything that he ever published". It was used frequently after this time by De Worde, and affords us towards the end of the century one of the most useful date-tests for undated books. Between May, 1497, and January, 1498, part of the cap of the soldier who stands on the right of the cross was broken away, so that any book containing this cut with the cap entire must be before 1498. In 1499 the cut began to split, and in 1500 it split right across. Towards the end of 1500 one of the two border lines at top and bottom was cut away. Of course there are for De Worde's books many date-tests, and when they can be worked in various ways and in conjunction, the result may be taken as very fairly accurate. If it were only possible to get once together all the scattered undated books for comparison, they could easily be arranged in their exact order.

In 1495 appeared the *Vitas Patrum*, "the moste vertuouse hystorye of the deuoute and right renowned lyves of holy faders lyvynge in deserte, worthy of remembraunce to all wel dysposed persones, whiche hath be translated out of Frenche into Englisshe by Wylliam Caxton of Westmynstre, late deed, and fynysshed at the laste daye of his lyff". The delay in the bringing out of this work may be due to the large number of illustrations, for it is profusely illustrated; the cuts, however, are very rudely designed and engraved.

In the Pepysian Library at Cambridge is a unique edition of the *Introductorium linguæ latinæ*, edited very likely by Horman, which has the words in the preface, " Nos sumus in anno salutis Millesimo quadringentesimo nonagesimo quinto (1495)," which I certainly take to be the year of printing, especially as another edition of the same book in the Bodleian, also unique, has the last word of the date, quinto, altered to nono, and must have been printed before July, 1499. The small tracts printed from 1495 to 1497 are very difficult to date with any precision, but there are a few of particular interest which may be ascribed to that period, such books, for instance, as the *Information for Pilgrims to the Holy Land*, a work well worth reading for amusement, which cannot be said of many of these books; Fitzjames's *Sermo die lune in ebdomada Pasche*, the *Sermo pro episcopo puerorum*, the *Mirror of Consolation*, and the *Three Kings of Cologne*.

1496 is the year usually ascribed to the edition of Trevisa's translation of the *De proprietatibus rerum* of Bartholomæus Anglicus, and I quoted earlier four lines of verse saying that Caxton had printed the book in Latin at Cologne. The three last lines of the same stanza referring to another matter are also very interesting. Having spoken of Caxton it continues :—

> And John Tate the yonger, joye mote he broke
> Whiche late hathe in Englond doo make this paper thynne
> That now in our englyssh this boke is prynted inne.

The watermark of this paper is an eight-pointed star in a circle. The supply of this paper does not appear to have been kept up for long, for I have only found it in two other English books. The Bartholomæus contains some very good woodcuts, finer than others of the period, and the press-work seems rather more regular than usual, so that perhaps we may accept the statement of Dibdin that "Of all the books printed in this country in the fifteenth century, the present one is the most curious and elaborate, and probably the most beautiful for its typographical execution". It is only fair to say, however, that the copy described by Dibdin was a very exceptional one. In 1496 also came out a reprint of the well-known *Book of St Alban's*, as it is generally called, a treatise on hunting, hawking, and heraldry, with the addition in this issue of the delightful chapter on fishing with an angle, our earliest printed treatise on the art. There is a woodcut of the angler at the beginning, and we see him busily at work with a large tub beside him, just like the German fisher of to-day, into which he may put his fish and keep them alive.

This book would naturally appeal especially to the richer class, and De Worde not only took especial pains with it, but struck off copies upon vellum, some of which have come down to our own day. From a typographical point of view the book is of great interest, for it is printed throughout in a foreign type which made its appearance in England on this occasion only. It was used first at Gouda by Gotfried van Os, but he seems to have discarded it about 1490 when he removed to Copenhagen. Besides acquiring this fount De Worde also obtained a number of woodcut capital letters, which are used in all his earliest books, and one or two woodcuts, which he used frequently until they were broken and worn out. It has always been a puzzle to me why, if De Worde had had this fount of type beside him for several years, he never used it before, and why, having used it this once, he never used it again. Not a single letter ever appears in another book, and yet the type is a very handsome one.

1498 saw the issue of three fine folios: the *Morte d' Arthur* of which the only known copy is in the John Rylands Library at Manchester, the *Golden Legend* of which the only known perfect copy is in the same library, and lastly the *Canterbury Tales* of Chaucer. The only perfect copy of this book was sold lately in the Ashburnham sale for £1000, and is now also in Manchester, though not, I regret to say, in the John Rylands Library. The first of these three books, the *Morte d'Arthur*, is a reprint of Caxton's edition, but it differs from it in having illustrations. These are no doubt of native workmanship, and might be justly described as the worst ever put into an English book, being coarsely drawn, badly designed, and incompetently engraved. The *Golden Legend* is a mere reprint of the earlier editions, but is interesting for two points in the colophon. The first is an example of the carelessness of the printers. The words in the earlier editions run, "Thus endeth the legend named in latin legenda aurea, that is to say in Englysshe the golden legende, for lyke as golde passeth all other metals, so this legende exceedeth all other books, wherein be contained all the high and great feasts of our lord" and so on. In this edition a line has been omitted, and the words run, "For like as golde passeth all other metalles, wherein ben contained all the highe and grete festes of our lord". Now although the omission makes nonsense of the whole sentence, it is reprinted exactly the same in the later editions issued by De Worde and Julian Notary.

The other point is the date in the colophon, which runs, "Fynysshed at Westmynster, the viii day of Janeuer, the yere of oure lorde (a) Thousande . cccc. lxxxxviii. And in the xiii year of the reygne of kynge Henry the VII". Now as the 13th year of Henry VII. ran from August 22, 1497, to August 21, 1498, it is clear that De Worde in speaking of January 8, 1498, meant 1498 as we would calculate, and not 1499, and therefore that he began his year on the 1st of January and not on the 25th of March, a most important point to be settled in arranging dated books. Another later proof as to De Worde's dating may be mentioned. In the tracts which he printed between January 1 and March 25, 1509, he speaks of himself as printer to the king's mother, but after Henry VIII. succeeded in 1509 he styles himself printer to the king's grandmother, so that he clearly used our method of dating.

About the year 1498, De Worde introduced his second device, the largest of the three used in the fifteenth century. It is almost square, with a broad border, and having Caxton's mark and initials above a flowering plant.

Between July and December, 1499, a series of small nicks were cut all round the outside edge, and this gives us a useful clue to checking the dates of several books.

In 1499, De Worde brought out an edition of *Mandeville's Travels*. It was not the first edition published in England by a year or two, but it was the first with illustrations, and most realistic illustrations they are. No doubt it was a very popular book, and the two copies known, one in the Cambridge University Library, the other at Stonyhurst, are both imperfect. Fortunately by means of the two we can obtain an exact collation. This year seems to have been a very busy one. While the dated books in the other years of the fifteenth century never rise above four, in this year there are ten, and a considerable number of undated books can be assigned to this year as well. Among them a number of small poetical pieces by Lidgate, reprints of Caxton's editions. One of these reprints shows how careless a printer W. de Worde was. He reprints the *Horse, the Shepe, and the Ghoos*, from a copy of Caxton's wanting a leaf, but never noticing anything wrong prints straight ahead, making of course nonsense of the whole.

All De Worde's quarto tracts were got up in the same style, the title at the top of the first leaf printed in one of Caxton's types, below this a woodcut not always very apposite to the subject of the work. There were two stock cuts of masters with large birches and their pupils seated before them, one of these being among the material obtained from Gotfried van Os. These of course were suitable for grammars and school books. Caxton's cuts for the Sarum Horae, the Crucifixion, The tree of Jesse, the three rioters and three skeletons, the rich man and Lazarus, and David and Bathsheba, came in very useful for theological books. The only special cut, that is one specially cut for the particular book and not belonging to a series, that I have found, is that on the title of the *Rote or mirror of consolation*, which depicts seven persons kneeling before an altar, above which two angels hold a monstrance.

At the end of the year 1500, De Worde moved from Westminster into Fleet Street at the sign of the Sun, the earliest book from the new address being dated May, 1501. This from the point of view of the bibliographer was an extremely well-timed move, for we can at once put all books with the Westminster imprint as before 1501, and all with the London one after 1500, thus dividing clearly the fifteenth and sixteenth century books. At the time of his moving he seems to have got rid of a considerable portion of his stock; some seems to have been destroyed and some sold, for many cuts which had belonged to De Worde or to Caxton are found afterwards in books printed by Julian Notary. De Worde seems to have been a successful business man, for when he moved into Fleet Street he occupied two houses close to St. Bride's Church, one his dwelling-house and the other a printing office, for which he paid the very high tithe rent of sixty-six shillings and eightpence.

The number of books printed by Wynkyn de Worde in the fifteenth century, counting in different editions of the same book, is 109, and of a considerable number of these only a single copy is known. It would seem probable that the printer, when issuing a small book, printed only a small number of copies, preferring to set up the type for a new edition rather than burden himself with much unsaleable stock. And it is curious how these various editions have been accidentally preserved. Only two copies are known of a book called the *Rote or mirror of consolation*, printed by De Worde in the fifteenth century, one of them is in the Pepysian library, the other in Durham Cathedral. Yet these two are of quite different editions, the one at Durham being certainly about 1496, the other certainly after the middle of 1499. Of the *Three Kings of Cologne* we have two editions, though only three copies are known. Indeed, for some time it was thought that each copy represented a different edition, as the copy in the British Museum, evidently bound up separately out of a volume of tracts, had had the last page of the tract preceding it bound in in place of the correct title-page.

Looking at the very large number of small books which De Worde printed between the end of 1496 and 1500, it is surprising how many are known from single copies. I have kept for many years a register of all the copies of early English books which are to be found anywhere, and taking the quartos printed by W. de Worde, which number altogether 68, I find that out of that number 47, that is more than two-thirds, are known to us now from single copies or fragments. And I feel certain that we owe the preservation of the majority of these to a cause we are now doing our best to destroy. A few worthy people centuries ago made collections of these tracts and bound them up in immensely stout volumes, which gave them an air of importance in themselves, and tended to preserve the tracts inside in a much better manner than if bound separately. I do not think I am exaggerating when I say that a hundred and fifty of the rarest that De Worde printed during his whole life can be traced to have been bound up in about twelve volumes at the beginning of this century. Some twenty-two of the rarest of W. de Worde's in the Heber Library came to him in one volume. Thirteen unique tracts which sold at the Roxburghe sale for £538, were in a single volume when the Duke purchased them fourteen years before for £26. I need only refer you to the University Library, a large number of whose unique Caxton and De Worde tracts came in three or four volumes. Then again, when so many are known only from fragments or single copies we may imagine what a large number have absolutely disappeared.

Some have been lost of late years or have disappeared since they were described. Three unique W. de Worde books of the fifteenth century were supposed to have perished in a fire in Wales early this century, but fortunately they had been sold by the owner of the library a short time before the fire. Others seem to have drifted into libraries whose owners know nothing about them. There is a unique De Worde printed before 1501, entitled the "*Contemplacyon or meditacyon of the shedynge of the blood of our lorde Jhesu Cryste at seven tymes*". This was seen and described by Herbert, who very likely saw it when it was sold at the Fletewode sale in 1774. Since then we have no record of the book, and though every year more information about private collections is published I can come upon no trace of it.

Beside the genuine books which have disappeared, by this I mean books which have been described by a trustworthy bibliographer, there are others which may reasonably be supposed to have existed, and one clue to these is afforded by the woodcuts. W. de Worde for example had certain series of cuts, specially made for certain books; but when he wished to decorate the title-page of a small tract, which was not itself to be otherwise illustrated, he used an odd cut out of his sets. Now when we can trace in different tracts odd cuts, manifestly belonging to a series, we may reasonably suppose that the book to which those series actually belong must have been printed.

To give a couple of instances. In the unique copy of Legrand's *Book of good manners* in the University Library without date, but printed about the middle of 1498, are two cuts, which really belong to a series made to illustrate the *Seven wise masters of Rome*. These cuts are fairly accurate copies of those used by Gerard Leeu in his edition of 1490. At a considerable later date De Worde did issue an edition of the *Seven wise masters*, illustrated with the series of which the two mentioned above formed part, and showing at that time marks of wear. Now as De Worde had the series cut by the beginning of 1498, I think it most probable that an edition of the book was then issued, for it is unlikely that he would go to the trouble of cutting the set unless he was preparing to print the book.

Again before the end of the fifteenth century De Worde had a series to illustrate *Reynard the Fox*. One cut is found on the first leaf of an edition of Lidgate's *The Horse, the sheep, and the goose*, in the University Library, another on the title-page of Skelton's *Bowge of Court* in the Advocates' Library at Edinburgh. In the collection of the University Librarian is a fragment of an edition of Reynard, evidently printed by W. de Worde about 1515, and this contains a third cut agreeing absolutely in size, in workmanship, and in style with the other two.

In this case again it seems probable that an edition illustrated with these cuts appeared before 1500.

The last press at Westminster during the fifteenth century is that of Julian Notary, which while it started in London about 1496 and only moved to Westminster in 1498, is more suitably taken in this place on account of its connexion with Wynkyn de Worde.

The first book issued was an edition of *Albertus de modis significandi*, printed in a neat Gothic type, but containing no information in its colophon beyond that it was printed in London at St. Thomas the Apostle's, probably close to the church of that name, and not at a house with that sign. There is also a printer's mark containing three sets of initials, I. N. for Julian Notary, I. B. for Jean Barbier, and I. H. for someone unidentified, but who there are some reasons for supposing to have been Jean Huvin, a printer at Rouen, who was associated in the production of books for the English market.

In 1497 the same printers issued an edition of the *Horae ad usum Sarum*, very neatly printed, and with delicate borders round the pages. All that remains of the book is a fragment of four pages, rescued from a book-binding, but this luckily contains the colophon, telling us that it was printed at St. Thomas the Apostle's, for W. de Worde. This book also contains the device with the three sets of initials.

In 1498 appeared a Sarum Missal, the first edition printed in England, and though otherwise well got up, the musical parts have the drawback of being without notes, only the staves having been printed, though whether this was done by design or merely because the printers had no musical type remains unknown. From the colophon of the Missal we learn that the printers, Julian Notary and Jean Barbier, had settled at Westminster, and had printed the book at the command and expense of W. de Worde. On the last leaf is Caxton's device, and on the title-page that of the printers. Of this book five copies are known, and of the four I have examined, the copy in the University Library is the only perfect one. About the fifth, belonging to the Duke of Sutherland, I have no information.

I. H. it is clear had left the firm, and though the printers use the same device as before, the initials I. H. have been cut out of it.

In 1499 Jean Barbier also disappeared, for in the edition of the *Liber festivalis* and *Quattuor Sermones* which appeared in that year the printer's mark has again been altered. All initials have been cut out and the name Julianus Notarii inserted in type. This form of the name suggests that he was not a notary as is generally stated, but the son of one. I have never been able to see a perfect copy of this book though Herbert describes one which he said was in the Inner Temple Library, but my inquiries there met with no success. Hain in his *Repertorium Bibliographicum* mentions a copy which seems not to be the one noticed by Herbert.

In April, 1500, Notary printed a most minute edition of the *Horæ ad usum Sarum*, it is in 64's as regards folding, and a printed page measures an inch and a quarter by an inch. Only a fragment of it is known, a quarter sheet containing sixteen leaves, but that luckily contains the colophon. It was very likely copied from another edition of the same size, which was printed at Paris the year before, but this point cannot be determined, as the only copy of the latter which existed was burnt with the greater part of the Offor collection. All we know now of it is the meagre note in the auctioneer's catalogue, "imperfect, but has end with imprint"—and he has not given the imprint!

The colophon of Notary's *Horae* tells us that it was printed in King Street, Westminster. King Street is the short street at the bottom of Whitehall in a straight line between Westminster Abbey and the Foreign Office. Lewis, in his life of Caxton, says that Caxton's printing office was in King Street, but I do not know of any reason for his assertion.

The last of Notary's books printed at Westminster is an edition of Chaucer's *Love and complaintes between Mars and Venus*, with some other pieces. This rare little book, having passed through the collections of Farmer, the Duke of Roxburghe, Sir Masterman Sykes and Heber, is now at Britwell. The colophon runs: "This imprynted in westmoster in King Street. For me Julianus Notarii." In spite of the word For, I think the book was printed by Julian Notary himself. It contains two cuts, reversed copies of two of Caxton's.

At what time Notary left Westminster cannot at present be settled, but probably almost immediately after W. de Worde. When his next dated book was issued in 1503 he had moved to London, and with his departure from King Street to Pynson's old house near Temple Bar printing ceased altogether in Westminster.

LECTURE II.

THE PRINTERS AT LONDON.

THE art of printing was introduced into London in 1480, three years after Westminster, two years after Oxford, and probably one year after St. Alban's, by a printer called Joannes Lettou. The name evidently denotes that he came orginally from Lithuania, of which the word Lettou is an old form. One thing is at once apparent when we come to examine his work, and that is that he was a skilled and practised printer, producing books entirely unlike Caxton's, and bearing every appearance of being the work of a foreign press. Where he learned to print it is impossible to find out, but whence his type was obtained no one can have the least doubt: it was certainly brought from Rome.

The type is identical with that used by a printer in Rome in 1478 and 1479, who really ought to have some connexion with English printing as his name was John Bulle. In his Roman books he describes himself as from Bremen. If it were possible to arrive at any explanation how a man from Bremen could be described as a Lithuanian, I should at once assume John Lettou and John Bulle to be identical, since the one apparently begins where the other leaves off. However, until some reasonable explanation is forthcoming it will be best to consider them as different people.

Lettou seems to have been assisted during the first two years of his career by a certain William Wilcock, but who this man may have been I have not been able to discover, unless he was a certain William Wilcock who is mentioned in the State Papers as having been presented to the living of Llandussell in 1487. The two books printed by Lettou were the *Questiones Antonii Andreae super duodecim libros metaphisice* and the *Expositiones super Psalterium* of Thomas Wallensis. Both these books are printed in a neat small Italian gothic, with two columns to the page and forty-nine or fifty lines in a column. The first of the two books, the *Antonius Andreae*, is a small folio of 106 leaves, and almost all the six known copies are imperfect. The book is very probably reprinted from the edition printed at Vicenza in 1477, the only earlier edition than the present, which, like it, is edited by Thomas Penketh. Penketh was a friar of the Augustinian house at Warrington, but went later as teacher of theology to Padua. He returned to Oxford in 1477, where he also taught theology, and was probably living there when his book was being printed at London.

The second of these two books is printed in exactly the same style and form as the first, with the exception of having fifty lines to the column in place of forty-nine. In the imprint the book is ascribed to the " Reverendissimus dominus Valencius," that is Jacobus Perez de Valentia, who was, however, not the author of this work, though he did write a commentary on the Psalms. The real author was a certain Thomas Wallensis or de Walleis. Henry Bradshaw, who discovered the mistake, gives the following explanation of it: "This edition is printed from an incomplete copy, and from the words of the colophon ' Reverendissimi domini Valencii,' the final s having been misread as an i, the work has been confounded with the commentary of Jacobus Perez de Valencia, which was printed at that place in 1484 and 1493. The v for w and the absence of the Christian name would also serve to create the confusion, or at any rate to perpetuate it."

Three editions of the indulgence of John Kendale were printed by Lettou in 1480. The first two have been preserved in a very curious manner. It was a common custom of the early binders to paste down the centre of each quire of paper a thin strip of vellum in order to prevent the thread which ran down the centre of the quire and stitched it to the bands of the binding from cutting through the paper. A copy of a foreign printed Bible, which appears to have been bound in England, perhaps by Lettou himself, and which is now in Jesus College Library, has the centre of each quire throughout the book lined with a strip of vellum, part of cut up copies of these two indulgences. Indulgences having their year printed upon them soon went out of date, and as they were of vellum and printed only on one side were very much used by bookbinders for lining bindings. These two indulgences were issued early in the year and have the date 1480, but no mention is made of the pontifical year of the pope. The third indulgence, also dated 1480, has besides, the date of the pontifical year, "the year of our pontificate the tenth," and as the popes dated like the kings, from the exact date of their accession or coronation, this copy must have been printed after August 7, 1480, on which date the tenth year of Sixtus IV. began.

After the printing of his two books and editions of the indulgence, Lettou entered into partnership with a printer called Wilhelmus de Machlinia, a native, as his name shows, of Mechlin in Belgium. Together they printed five books, the *Tenores Novelli* of Lyttelton, the *Abridgement of the Statutes*, and the *Year-books* of the thirty-third, thirty-fifth, and thirty-sixth years of Henry VI.

For these books the printers used a small very cramped black letter, abounding in abbreviations, and often difficult to read. It appears to have been designed after the law-hand of the period. The edition of the *Tenures* is the only one of these books with an imprint, and it contains the names of both printers, and the statement that the book was printed in the city of London, "juxta ecclesiam omnium sanctorum". There were, however, several churches in

London at this time dedicated to All Saints, and it is not possible now to settle which particular one was meant. Complete sets of these five books are in the British Museum and the University Library, Cambridge.

The complete change in the character of the books produced after Machlinia had joined Lettou shows that his strong point was legal printing, and during his continuance in business he seems to have printed all the law-books issued in England. But perhaps the most marked peculiarity of this partnership is the extraordinary deterioration in the books produced. The work of Lettou was marked by excellence of typography and the many improvements introduced by an evidently practised printer. As soon as Machlinia joined him the work became slovenly. It might almost be supposed that Mr. William Wilcock, who had defrayed the expense of Lettou's work, had either tried it as a speculation and found it a poor one, or had only wished the two books to be specially printed for his own use and had then left the printer to shift for himself. It is curious, too, that Lettou's neat type should have entirely disappeared. The real reason for this probably was that though it was very neat it had none of the abbreviations necessary in a type used for printing law-books.

While Lettou remained in the firm the work, though much deteriorated, retained a certain amount of regularity. All the books had signatures and were regular in size, though their appearance was not good. After the issue of these five books Lettou seems to have ceased printing, but the type was used for one more book, which it will be well to notice here, *The History of the Siege of Rhodes*. This was written in Latin by Gulielmus Caorsin, vice-chancellor of the Knights of Malta, and was translated into English by John Kay, who styles himself poet-laureat to Edward IV. It gives an account of the great victory of the Rhodians against the Turks and the death of Mahomet.

It is the only English printed book which we cannot definitely ascribe to any particular printer. By most early writers it was classed as a production of Caxton, and Dibdin places it under Caxton in his *Typographical Antiquities*, though he there expresses a doubt as to its being his work. "The typography," he says, "is so rude as to induce me to suppose that the book was not printed by Caxton. The oblique dash for the comma is very coarse; and the adoption of the colon and the period, as well as the comparatively wide distances between the lines, are circumstances which, as they are not to be found in Caxton's acknowleged publications, strongly confirm this supposition." Five years later, writing in the *Bibliotheca Spenceriana*, he seems to have settled more accurately. "I have very little doubt," he writes there, "of its having been executed by Lettou and Machlinia, or by the former of these printers, rather than by Caxton. The letters, however, great and small, especially the larger ones, and some of the compound smaller ones, bear a strong resemblance to the smallest types of our first printer; but on a comparison with those of the *Tenures* of Lyttelton and of the *Ancient Abridgement of the Statutes*, printed by Lettou and Machlinia, the resemblance is quite complete." The type is certainly that used by Lettou and Machlinia, and the considerable difference in appearance from the other five books is caused by the text being in English, which makes more difference than would be imagined, and also that there are very few of the abbreviations which crowd the other books. Then again the lines of type are spaced out, giving the page a much lighter appearance.

Though the dedication is to Edward IV. it does not necessarily follow that the book was printed before his death, for the early printers in reprinting a MS. would keep to the preface as there written. It might, however, have been printed as early as 1483, and immediately the law books had been completed. Who the printer was I do not think can ever be settled. When it was printed Machlinia had probably started by himself with his new types, and I do not think it can have been printed by Lettou, as it has not the signatures to the pages which he invariably used.

We may, I think, date the break up of the partnership of John Lettou and William de Machlinia about 1482-83, and from that date onwards Machlinia worked alone. He seems to have made a fresh start with new type, for he has at least three founts which had not been used before. The difficulties in the way of making any arrangement or arriving at any definite conclusions about his books are very great. We know that he printed at least twenty-two books, and not one single one is dated. Signatures, directors, headlines, seem to be present or absent without rule or reason. There is hardly any method of arranging the books in groups, every book stands alone in splendid isolation.

The only division possible is according to the type used in the books, and in this way we can separate them into two groups. Those of the first group are printed in two founts of a square gothic type, and as in the colophons of the two books in this series which possess them the printer speaks of himself as living near the " Flete-bridge," we call these books the ones printed in the Fleet-bridge type. The other group are in a regular English type, similar in general appearance to some of Caxton's or that used by the printer of St. Alban's, and in the imprint to one of these books Machlinia speaks of himself as printing in Holborn, so that we speak of this series of books as printed in the Holborn type. It is of course quite possible that the two addresses refer to the same place, and that Machlinia had but the one office, but with our present information it seems better to count the two addresses as different since it gives us a method of dividing the books.

It is probable that the Fleet-bridge group is the earlier, so we will take it first. In it there are altogether eight books. Three folios, the *Tenures of Lyttelton*, the *Nova Statuta*, and the *Promise of Matrimony*, four quartos, the *Vulgaria Terentii*, the *Revelation of St. Nicholas to a Monk of Evesham*, and two books by Albertus Magnus, the *Liber Aggregationis seu de secretis naturae*, and the *Secreta mulierum*, and one small book, probably a 16º, an edition of the *Horae ad usum Sarum*.

The two books of Albertus Magnus are certainly the most neatly printed, the press work being tidy and regular, which was not generally the case with this printer's productions.

The copy of the *Secreta mulierum* in the University Library is an interesting one, though, unfortunately, imperfect. On the first leaf which is blank there is a certain amount of writing, and amongst other things the following sentence: "Annus domini nunc est 1485 in anno Ricardi tercii 3º". This note, supposing it to have been written at the time to which it refers, and there is no reason to doubt it, must have been written between June 26 and August 22, 1485, showing that at any rate the book was printed before that date. The other book of Albertus Magnus, the *Liber aggregationis*, has a colophon stating that it was printed by "William de Machlinia in the most wealthy city of London, near the bridge vulgarly called the Flete-bridge". The wealth of London seems to have impressed the alien printer, for he always applies the word "*opulentissima*" to that city.

The small *Horae* we have little information about, for we know of its existence only from nineteen leaves scattered about the country. There are eight in Corpus Christi College, Oxford, seven in the British Museum, four in Lincoln Minster, and two in the University Library, Cambridge. These have all been extracted from bindings, and in the cases where we know the particular bindings from which they came these bindings were the work of the same man, whose initials were G. W. From the way in which the leaves were printed, and the way in which they were afterwards folded, a point too technical and difficult of description to touch on here, we may pretty safely say that the *Horae* was a 16º and not an 8º. It may be worth while remarking that the early printers used only the simple folding, which with each successive folding exactly halves the size of the previous one. The sheet folded into two leaves produced folio size, this folded again once made 4to, folded again 8º, again 16º, again 32º, and again 64º. The duodecimo or 12º, which depends on more complicated folding, was quite unknown.

The *Horae*, so far as we can see from what remains, contained no illustrations, but it had an engraved border which was used round the pages beginning certain portions of the book. This engraved border we afterwards find in Pynson's hands, and is the only definite link connecting him with this press. Bradshaw, in his paper on the " Image of Pity," suggests that Ames, who quoted this book in his *Typographical Antiquities*, had seen a complete copy, but as he describes it merely as "a book of devotions on vellum," and adds no particulars, I think that he simply described it from the few leaves in his own possession, which are now in the British Museum in the great so-called Bagford volumes of despoiled title-pages.

The *Revelation of St. Nicholas to a Monk of Evesham* is one of the most remarkable volumes of the fifteenth century, very well worth reading, for it is full of early English stories and allusions. (I may say in passing that Mr. Arber has issued a cheap reprint of it.) The story tells of a man who was taken through purgatory and was shown various people whom he had known or heard of and listened to their stories. It seems to me very curious that no other editions of the book were issued in early times, it seems exactly the kind of book which must have been popular. Typographically, the book is interesting as showing an excellent example of wrong imposition, that is that when the one side of the sheet had been printed, the other side was put down upon its form of type the wrong way round, and consequently the pages come all in their wrong order, page 1 being printed on the first side of the first leaf, page 14 follows it on the other side, then page 16, then page 4, and so on. Now, most printers who had done this stupid thing, and it was not an uncommon accident, would have destroyed the sheet and reprinted it. Not so Machlinia. He printed off some more copies of the wrong sheet and, cutting it up, pasted the four pages in their proper places. In one of the two known copies this has had unfortunate results, for some curious inquirer, noticing the pages pasted together, has tried to separate them to find out what was underneath, and they have suffered severely in the process.

The *Vulgaria Terentii* is the last of the quartos in this group. It is a book that was often printed, but of the present edition the copy in the University Library is the only one remaining, and it, unfortunately, is slightly imperfect.

Of the folios, the *Nova Statuta* is the most important, and also by far the commonest, for I have examined over a dozen copies myself, and I know of a good many more. The book must have been printed after April, 1483, as the subject-matter runs up to that date. The *Promise of Matrimony*, another folio in this type, consisting only of four leaves, relates to the agreement made in 1475 between Edward IV. and Louis XI. for the marriage of the Princess Elizabeth of York and Prince Charles, afterwards Charles VIII., King of France.

I have noticed that in nearly all the copies of the law books printed by Lettou and Machlinia, or Machlinia alone, that I have examined, the initial letters, which were filled in by hand in colour, appear to have been done by the same person; the letter roughly in red, and a twirl or two by way of ornament in pale green or blue. I suppose the subject of the books was so severely practical that unless this had been done before the book left the office it would never have been done at all. However, in English printing generally, though the spaces were left for fine initials, I can remember no book with them filled in in any but the plainest way, a contrast to the beautiful work so often found in Italian books.

The last group of books, which number fourteen, are called the Holborn type books, because in the imprint of one of the two books that contain them we find the words, "Enprente per moy william Maclyn en Holborn". The general type used for the text of these books is very remarkably like that used by Veldener at Utrecht and by John Brito at Bruges, and may, perhaps, have been obtained by Machlinia from abroad, though it is of the same school of type as several used in England.

The most important book issued in this series is an edition of the *Chronicles of England*. It is a very rare book, but there is an imperfect copy in Cambridge in the Barham collection in Pembroke College. The space for the initial letters, as is usually the case with early books, has been left blank to be filled in by the rubricator, but in one copy that I have seen, the initials have been filled in in gold, not gold leaf but gold paint, and this is the only example of its use that I have found in an early English book. Another curious point about the book is that though it is a folio, a folio of 238 leaves, yet in all copies leaves 59 and 66, the first and last leaves of a quire, are printed on quarto paper. I thought once that perhaps for some reason these leaves had been cancelled and reprinted, but it seems more probable that the printer had for the moment run out of his supply of ordinary-sized paper, and had to use some of a much larger size cut in half.

Three editions were published by Machlinia of the curious *Treatise on the Pestilence*, by Canutus or Kamitus, Bishop of Aarhaus in Denmark, and of each edition only one copy is known, one in the British Museum, one in the University Library, and one sold lately in the sale of the Ashburnham Library and now at Manchester. I must warn any one who uses Dibdin's *Typographical Antiquities*, that the facsimile page of the book which he gives is made up from the upper part of the first leaf of the Cambridge copy and the lower part of the same leaf of the Manchester copy, which he must have seen when it was in the possession of Triphook, the bookseller, so that the resulting facsimile is rather puzzling. The fact that one of these editions, that in the British Museum, has a title-page, makes us inclined to put it to rather a late date, but at any rate it is the earliest title-page in an English printed book.

Another book in this group, by far the commonest and best known, is the *Speculum Christiani*, ascribed to a writer named John Watton, a curious medley of theological matter interspersed with pieces of English poetry. The colophon states that the book was printed for and at the expense of a merchant named Henry Vrankenbergh. About this merchant I could find out nothing until, curiously enough, on my last visit to Cambridge a fortnight ago, my attention was drawn by a friend to a note in the Descriptive Catalogue of ancient deeds in the Record Office, where is a note of a "Demise to Henry Frankenbergk and Barnard van Stondo, merchants of printed books, of an alley in St. Clement's Lane, called St. Mark's Alley, 10th May, 1482".

This is, I believe, the earliest note relating to foreign stationers or merchants of printed books in England, but I hope from the same source we may expect to obtain many more as soon as the endless series of documents in the Rolls Office are calendared.

An edition of the *Vulgaria Terentii* was also printed in this type. An almost perfect copy was added to the British Museum Library two years ago, and a considerable portion of another copy is in the library of Caius College.

Machlinia also printed two of the *Nova Festa*, the *Festum visitationis beate Marie virginis* and the *Festum transfigurationis Jesu Christi*. The first of these is only known from two leaves which had been used to line the boards of the binding of Pynson's *Dives and Pauper*. Of the second a beautiful and perfect copy is in the library of the Marquis of Bath. It is curious to notice that it contains not only the feast according to the Sarum use, but also according to the Roman use.

The three last of Machlinia's books to be noticed are the three which, though undated themselves, contain certain evidences of date. The first of these contains the statutes made in the first year of Richard III., and, as this first year ran from June 26, 1483, to June 25, 1484, the book cannot be earlier than the second half of the latter year.

The second book is one about which I am very much inclined to doubt whether it was printed by Machlinia at all, but rather by Veldener, who used apparently identical type; and though I have had for several years under my charge at Manchester the only copy of the book known I cannot make up my mind about it. It is an edition of the *Regulae et ordinationes* of Innocent VIII., and could not at any rate have been printed before the very end of 1484. The type seems newer in appearance than any of Machlinia's, though to all appearance identical. Dibdin, with his usual readiness, helps us by remarking, "It presents us with the same character or general appearance of type as that which Caxton and Machlinia occasionally used. It is not much unlike the St. Alban's type."

The last production is a Bull of Innocent VIII. confirming the marriage of Henry VII. and Elizabeth of York. It was reissued in 1494 by Alexander VI., and there the date is given as 27th March, 1486.

Two copies of this Bull are known, one in the library of the Society of Antiquaries and one at Manchester. Herbert, in his *Typographical Antiquities*, describes a copy differing from these in having a concluding paragraph, apparently cut away from both the known copies.

Richard Pynson was by birth a native of Normandy, as we learn from his letters of denization, but practically nothing of his personal history is known. It is probable that he was educated at the University of Paris, for we find in a list of students in 1464 the name "Ricardus Pynson Normannus," and this may very well be the printer. It was, however, in Normandy that he learned to print, probably from Richard le Talleur, a noted printer of Rouen, as may be seen by certain small habits connected with printing which he fell into, and which are very typical of Rouen work.

Although we have only circumstantial evidence, evidence depending on a number of almost trifling details, to back up the statement, it seems now almost certain that Pynson succeeded Machlinia. My own impression is that he succeeded immediately on the death or retirement of the latter, with hardly any interval. A very strong reason for this impression is that had any long time elapsed between the cessation of Machlinia's press and the commencement of Pynson's, England would have been left without a printer who could set up law French. Caxton and Wynkyn de Worde were presumably unable to do it, at any rate they printed no books of the kind except some year-books of Henry VII., and it must be remembered that in Henry VII.'s reign for the first time the year-books were written in English. I do not mean to suggest that Pynson ever worked with Machlinia, but only that when the latter ceased to work Pynson came over and started in his place, perhaps taking over some of his printing material or even starting work in his old office. The engraved border which Machlinia had used in his *Sarum Horae*, the only piece of ornament he seems to have possessed, we find used afterwards by Pynson, and it is a very common thing to find Pynson's earliest bindings lined with waste leaves of Machlinia's printing. Had Pynson worked with Machlinia we should have expected the latter's founts of type to have passed into his hands, as Caxton's were inherited by Wynkyn de Worde, but they did not. Indeed they totally disappeared, and what we do find of Machlinia's in Pynson's hands is merely the refuse that we might expect a printer to find in an office just vacated by another. Had Pynson not been ready to take over the place this waste stuff would have been destroyed. The question is then, when did Machlinia cease or Pynson begin? I should say that Machlinia ceased much later than is supposed and Pynson began much earlier, and that the two events happened between 1488 and 1490. At first when Pynson arrived he was without material, so he commissioned Le Talleur at Rouen to print for him the two law books most in demand, *Lyttelton's Tenures* and *Statham's Abridgement of Cases* to the end of Henry VI.

Probably in 1490 to '91 he began printing on his own account. His first dated book was issued in November, 1492, but five books, if not more, can be placed earlier; these are an edition of Chaucer's *Canterbury Tales*, a *Latin Grammar*, a poetical book, and two or more *Year-books*. The Chaucer is a particularly fine book, printed in two sizes of type, a larger for the poetry, and a smaller for the prose which is printed in two columns. It is also illustrated with a set of woodcuts illustrating the different pilgrims. It is interesting to notice that these cuts were altered in some cases while the book was passing through the press in order to serve as the portrait of another pilgrim. The serjeaunt with a little alteration becomes the doctor of physick, the squire becomes the manciple. There has been a good deal of controversy as to the date of the printing of this book and whether it could have appeared before Caxton's death in the latter part of the year 1491. Pynson in his prologue, which is rather confused and difficult to understand, says, speaking of Chaucer: "Of whom I among alle other of his bokes, the boke of the tales of Canterburie, in whiche ben many a noble historie of wisdome policie mirth and gentilnes. And also of vertue and holynes whiche boke diligently ovirsen and duely examined by the pollitike reason and ouirsight of my worshipful master William Caxton accordinge to the entent and effecte of the seid Geffrey Chaucer and by a copy of the seid master Caxton purpos to imprent, by ye grace, ayde, and supporte of almighty god." I think had Caxton been dead Pynson would have alluded to it in some way, speaking of him, perhaps, as "my late worshipful master" or "my worshipful master late dead". The term worshipful master does not imply that Pynson had been an apprentice or assistant to Caxton, but was merely a courteous way of referring to the printer and editor whose work he was about to reprint. Blades, in his life of Caxton, speaks of Pynson's having used Caxton's device, but this mistake has arisen through a made-up book in the British Museum, a copy of Bonaventure's *Speculum vite Christi*. The copy wanted the end, and some former owner, in order to make the book look more complete, has added a leaf with Caxton's device printed on it.

The *Latin Grammar* is known only from three leaves, one in the Bodleian and two in the British Museum. The leaf in the Bodleian appears from an inscription upon it to have been used to line a binding as early as 1494. The book was printed entirely in the large black type of the *Chaucer*, the first of Pynson's types, and which he does not appear to have used after 1492.

Another book printed about this time was a book of poetry of a quarto size. All that is at present known of this book are two little strips making part of a leaf, and each containing six lines of verse, three on each side. I found these fragments a year or two ago amongst a bundle of uncatalogued leaves in the Bodleian, but I have not been able to determine from what book they come. The story is apparently of some one who having been in purgatory is allowed to revisit the world in order to warn others of what he had seen there. This was a common story, and is found in many forms, and it is very probable that the fragments belong to some version of a work of this class called *Spiritus Guidonis*.

The two other books in this series are two year-books, for the first and ninth years of Edward IV. All these early books, with the exception, of course, of the poetry fragments, contain Pynson's first device, which consists of his monogram in white upon a black background, not at all unlike in style that used by Le Talleur at Rouen, with whom he had been associated. When the device was used in November, 1492, a small alteration had been made in it, so that from the state of the device as well as by the type used we are able to settle which books belong to this earliest group.

In 1492 Pynson's first dated book appeared, an edition of the *Doctrinale* of Alexander Grammaticus, editions of which had already been printed abroad in considerable numbers. Pynson's was not copied from any of these, having a different commentary, but who this commentary is by I have not yet been able to ascertain.

This book was only discovered quite lately, and I came upon it by a fortunate accident. The owner, or rather guardian, of it happened to have read in some book that the earliest dated book of Pynson's was issued in 1493. Knowing that he had an earlier one he wrote to the British Museum about it, and I heard casually that the book had been sent to them to examine. I went up to London immediately to see if I could see the book, but was told it had been returned, nor could I obtain any information as to where it was to be found. Luckily, the owner was so far interested as to write a note to one of the papers mentioning the existence of the book, and also the place where it was preserved —the Grammar School at Appleby. The following Saturday I set off to Appleby, and had the pleasure of examining it at my leisure. It is a beautiful copy, quite perfect, in its original binding, and, as one would have hoped, with end leaves taken from Machlinia's *Chronicle*. It has a perfectly clear Latin imprint which runs: "And thus ends the commentary of the Doctrinale of Alexander, printed by me Richard Pynson of the parish of St Clement Danes outside the bar of the new Temple at London the 13th day of the month of November in the year of the incarnation of our Lord 1492". From this colophon it is clear that if Pynson did commence work in Machlinia's old office, which was in Holborn, he had by this time removed to other premises. The commentary in the book is printed in a very small neat type which Pynson had probably had made for him abroad, as it contained no w. I am sorry to say that the discovery of this book has thrown out of order the list of Pynson's types which I gave in the introduction to my *Facsimiles of Early English Printing*.

In 1493 appeared Henry Parker's *Dialogue of Dives and Pauper*, which was always considered, before the discovery of the *Doctrinale*, Pynson's first dated book. It is printed in a new and handsome type, and this is the only dated book in which it is used, though there are four undated quartos in the same type, which may be put down to the same year. These are the *Festum nominis Jesu*, one of the *Nova Festa* printed as supplements to the *Sarum Breviary*. The *Life of St. Margaret*, Lidgate's *Churl and Birde*, and an edition apparently of some statutes or a similar work known from two leaves in the library at Lambeth. Of the *Festum nominis Jesu* one copy is known, bound up in a volume with several other tracts, among them being Caxton's

Festum transfigurationis Jesu Christi. It was for a while in the Congregational Library in London but was eventually sold to the British Museum. Three printed leaves from the beginning of the poem amongst the fragments in the Bodleian are all that remain of the *Life of St. Margaret*. The Lidgate's *Churl and Birde* after passing through the sales of Willett, the Marquis of Blandford, Sir F. Freeling and B. H. Bright, passed with the Grenville Library into the British Museum.

Two editions of Mirk's *Liber festivalis*, each known from a single copy, one in the Pepysian Library, the other in the University Library, belong probably to this time. The various changes in the book are interesting to trace. In the earliest editions there are no references to, or additional chapters for, the new feasts which were then coming into use; then come editions with the extra feasts printed together at the end as a kind of supplement to the book, and finally we get the editions with these extra feasts put into their proper places in the body of the book. The edition in the Pepysian Library is without these extra feasts, while that in the University Library has them as a supplement of ten leaves at the end. In the next edition, which was printed about the end of 1493 by W. de Worde, the feasts have been incorporated into their proper places.

In 1494 Pynson reverts to his earlier types and issued a translation by Lidgate from Boccaccio called the *Falle of Princes*, remarkable for its charming woodcuts. In this book, for the first time, Pynson used his second device, a large woodcut, containing his initials on a black shield with a helmet above on which is perched a small bird. This I imagine is meant for a finch, a punning allusion to his name, since Pynson is the Norman name for a finch. Round the whole is a border of flowering branches, in which are birds and grotesque beasts. This device supplies us later with a most useful date test, for the edge split in 1496 and the piece broke off entirely towards the end of 1497.' Probably in this year (1494) Pynson issued his edition of the *Speculum vitae Christi*, of which an almost perfect copy is in King's Library. It is illustrated with a large number of neat woodcuts, which are copied more or less from Caxton's illustrations to the same book, though they are by no means identical with them, as has been often stated. As a general rule Pynson's cuts are of very much better execution and design than either Caxton's or De Worde's, and though not in all cases good, as for instance in the *Canterbury Tales*, yet they never sink to the very bad drawing and engraving so often found in the works of the other two printers.

The year 1495, so far as dated books go, was an entire blank, and 1496 was hardly better, having only the two grammars, the *Liber synonymorum* and *Liber equivocorum*, both usually attributed to Joannes de Garlandia, but many undated books of very considerable interest appeared about this time. Two of these, the *Epitaph of Jasper, Duke of Bedford*, and the *Foundation of our Ladies' Chapel at Walsingham* are to be found in the Pepysian Library. Jasper Tudor, Duke of Bedford, and half-brother of Henry VI., died on December 21, 1495, and the book must have been printed early in 1496. It is supposed to be written by one Smarte, the keeper of the hawks to the Duke, and begins as follows:—

> Rydynge al alone with sorowe sore encombred
> In a frosty fornone, faste by Severnes syde
> The wordil beholdynge, whereat much I wondred
> To se the see and sonne to kepe both tyme and tyde.
> The ayre ouer my hede so wonderfully to glyde
> And how Saturne by circumference borne is aboute
> Whiche thynges to beholde, clerely me notyfyde
> One verray god to be, therin to haue no dowte.

The end runs:—

> Kynges prynces moste souerayne of renoune
> Remembre oure maister that gone is byfore

> This worlde is casual, nowe up nowe downe
> Wherfore do for your silfe, I can say no more
> Honor tibi Deus, gloria et laus
> Qd' Smerte maister de ses ouzeaus.

This poem has been attributed to Skelton, though I do not know for what reason. On the title-page is a special cut, not used elsewhere, of Smarte kneeling, with his hawk on his wrist, and presenting with his other hand a book to a person standing. The *Foundation of our Ladies' Chapel at Walsingham* is a small tract relating to the priory of the Augustinian canons of St. Mary, once one of the most important places of pilgrimage in England, and which was described by Erasmus. The first leaf, which would have contained the title, is wanting, but the text begins on the second:—

> Of this chapell se here the fundacyon
> Bylded the yere of crystes incarnacyon
> A thousande complete, sixty and one
> The tyme of Sent Edward kyng of this region.

About this time appeared the first English edition of *Mandeviles Travels*, the only edition, I think, issued without illustrations, and a little reprint of Caxton's *Art and Craft to Know Well to Die*, of which the only known copy, formerly Radcliffe's, is in the Hunterian Museum at Glasgow.

Another poetical tract is the *Life of Petronylla*, beginning:—

> The parfite lyfe to put in remembraunce
> Of a virgyn moost gracious and entere
> Which in all vertu had souereyn suffysaunce
> Called Petronylla petyrs doughter dere.

This little tract consists of four leaves, and though only two copies are known at present it is probable that more are in existence, for the book seems to occur in all the sales of large libraries which have occurred within the last hundred years.

About 1496 Henry Quentell, a Cologne printer, had issued the first edition of the *Expositio Hymnorum et Sequentiarum*, according to the use of Sarum, but it was found that several hymns and sequences were omitted, so Pynson issued two supplements, one of sixteen leaves to the hymns, another of six to the sequences.

Another rather quaint book issued about this time is a kind of vocabulary or phrase book in English and French. " Here is a good book to lerne to speak french, Vecy ung bon liure a apprendre a parler fraunchoys." The book contains also specimens of letters in French relating to trade, in fact it was evidently intended as a manual for people who had business relations with France.

Two more editions of the *Nova Festa*, the *Festum transfigurationis* and the *Festum nominis Jesu* were issued about this time. The only copies known of these two books are in a private library in Norfolk, and I have not yet had an opportunity of examining them.

In 1497, or perhaps slightly earlier, Pynson began to use his third device, made probably to take the place of the second which had split, and taking warning from it he had the new one cut in metal. The device consists of the shield and monogram supported by a man and a woman, with the helmet and bird above. The border, which is cut on a separate piece, contains birds and foliage, with the Virgin and Child and a saint in the bottom corners. In the lowest part of the frame a piece in the form of a ribbon has been cut out for the insertion of type. In consequence of the weakness of that particular place the small piece of border below the ribbon began to be pushed inwards, and by 1499 there was a distinct indentation in the border. This got deeper and deeper year by year, until the piece broke off entirely in 1513. The first dated book in which it occurs is an edition of Alcock's *Mons perfectionis*, but it occurs in several of the undated books that can be placed about 1496.

Towards the end of 1497 Pynson issued the plays of Terence, the first classic (with the exception of an Oxford edition of the *Pro Milone*, which is known from a few leaves) that had been printed in England. The six plays were evidently issued separately and not as a volume, for they differ considerably typographically. There is some difficulty, too, in determining in what order they were issued.

In 1498 there are seven dated books, one of them being the sermon of Bishop Alcock called *Gallicantus*, and he is so pleased with jesting on his name that he prefaces the text of his sermon with a little black picture of a cockerel, which he also used as a device. Another edition of the *Doctrinale* of Alexander the Grammarian was issued this year, but I have not yet seen the book as the only copy known belongs to Lord Beauchamp.

In 1499 a very interesting book was printed by Pynson, this was the *Promptorius Puerorum*, a Latin-English dictionary ascribed to a monk of Lynn. The imprint tells us that the book was printed for Frederick Egmondt and Peter post pascha. Frederick Egmondt was an important stationer, and no doubt Peter post pascha was a stationer also, though what name in the vernacular can be represented by post pascha remains an unsolved riddle. Mr. Albert Way, in his edition of the *Promptorium parvulorum*, applies a curious amount of misplaced ingenuity to the question of the identity of these two stationers. "We find about the time in question," he says, speaking of the name Egmondt, "a distinguished person of that family, possibly the patron of Pynson, Frederic, son of William IV., Count of Egmond. In 1472 he received from his uncle, the Duke of Gueldres, the lordship of Buren; he was named governor of Utrecht by the Archduke Maximilian in 1492; two years later Buren was raised to a count in reward of his services. There was a Peter, an illegitimate brother of his father, who might have been living at that time; what was his surname does not appear." Another book printed about this year was the *Elegantiarum viginti praecepta*, a book which I am fond of for a peculiar reason. I found once a leaf of it in the Signet Library, Edinburgh, and, not knowing that any copy was in existence, set to work to reconstruct the book from the leaf. I counted the lines, and, comparing with foreign editions, conjectured the size and structure of the book, and knowing how Pynson would make a title-page with a woodcut, and the woodcut he would probably use, I made up a description of the book, taking the title from an early bibliography. At last I heard of a perfect copy in a private library which the owner was kind enough to allow me to examine. When the book arrived I found I had not only got the collation right, but by a lucky inspiration had selected the correct woodcut for the title-page. As it happens I might have spared myself the trouble, for I found afterwards a fairly accurate collation of the book in an authority I had not consulted.

A curious prognostication for 1499 is in the Bodleian. It is addressed to Henry VII., and was drawn out by a William Parron, who lived at Piacenza and called himself doctor of medicine and professor of astrology. Another prognostication for 1502, by the same author, was printed by Pynson, and some fragments are in the Library of Westminster Abbey. He also wrote an astrological work on Henry, Duke of York, afterwards Henry VIII., in 1502, of which there are MSS. in the British Museum and Bibl. Nationale, but it does not seem ever to have been printed.

The *Morton Missal* which Pynson printed in 1500 is perhaps the finest book printed in the fifteenth century in England. It was produced at the expense of Cardinal Morton whose arms appear at the beginning, and Pynson has introduced into the borders and initials a rebus on the name consisting of the letters Mor surmounting a barrel or tun. Five copies of this book are known, three being on vellum.

One of the latter copies, slightly imperfect, is in the library of Trinity College. In the copy at Manchester all the references to St. Thomas and his service, which had been scraped out and erased according to the command of Henry VIII., have been entirely filled in by some pious seventeenth century owner in gold.

In the imprint, after setting forth that the book was printed at the command of Cardinal Morton, Pynson adds the date, January 10, 1500. Now, as Cardinal Morton died on September 15, 1500, I think we have here a strong piece of evidence that Pynson, like De Worde, began his year on January 1. For if he had begun it on March 25, then January 10, 1500, would be after the Cardinal was dead, and Pynson would surely have spoken of him as lately dead, or in some way alluded to the loss of his patron.

The *Book of Cookery*, belonging to the Marquis of Bath, was also printed this year. It begins: "Here beginneth a noble boke of festes royalle and cokery, a boke for a pryncis housholde or any other estates, and the makynge therof accordynge as ye shall fynde more playnly within this boke". Then follows an account of certain great banquets, the feast at the coronation of Henry V.; "the earle of Warwick's feast to the king, the feast of my lorde chancellor archbishop of York at his stallacion in York," and so on. After the account of the feasts comes the more practical Calendar of Cookery.

Two editions of the *Informatio Puerorum*, a small grammatical work founded upon the *Donatus*, were issued about this time. In the colophon of one it is stated that the book was printed for George Chasteleyn and John Bars. I have found no reference anywhere to John Bars, but George Chasteleyn was an Oxford bookseller, carrying on business at the Sign of St. John the evangelist in that city. It was for him also that in 1506 Pynson printed an edition of the *Principia* of Peregrinus de Lugo. About this time there was no press in Oxford, so that books for use in the schools there had to be printed in London.

In a scrap-book in the British Museum are some leaves of an edition of the romance of *Guy of Warwick*, which may be ascribed to Pynson, and they are printed in a curious mixture of his early types. These leaves were discovered in 1860 in the binding of a copy of Maydeston's *Directorium Sacerdotum*, printed by Pynson in 1501, and an account of them was sent by their discoverer, who signs himself E. F. B., to *Notes and Queries*. Now, of this edition of the *Directorium*, only two copies are known, one in the British Museum and one in Ripon Cathedral, and I should very much like to know from which copy these leaves were obtained.

During all the period from 1490 to 1500 Pynson was busy issuing editions of law books, more than a quarter of his productions being of this class, and it is probable that a considerable number more printed in the fifteenth century may yet be discovered. They are not of a nature to attract much interest, and are generally very badly catalogued, or catalogued in collections and not separately, and in one great English library at least they have no more detailed press mark than Law Room, so it is needless to say I have not yet examined such books as they may have in that library.

Though he did not print so many books as De Worde in the fifteenth century, nevertheless Pynson was evidently a more enterprising and careful printer. He had seven distinct founts of type, all of which were made for him and not inherited from other printers, and the works he produced were of a much more scholarly nature, though this becomes more apparent in his work during the sixteenth century. His patrons were often learned and distinguished men, for whom he produced such splendid work as the *Morton Missal*, and he became later the recognised king's printer. In the fifteenth century he printed altogether eighty-two books.

Pynson, like De Worde, very considerately moved to a new address at the end of the century, previous to 1501 he was in St. Clement's parish, outside Temple Bar, which was the limit, I think, of the parish, but afterwards moved inside Temple Bar, where he carried on business at the Sign of the George. The colophon to the *Book of Cookery*, printed in 1500, says, "Imprinted without Temple Bar"; the colophon to the *Directorium Sacerdotum* of 1501 says, "intra barram novi templi," so that the date is pretty accurately fixed.

LECTURE III.

THE STATIONERS.

In speaking of the history of the printed book in the fifteenth century I have so far dealt only with the printers of London and Westminster; to-day I propose to touch on the books printed abroad for the English market and the stationers who sold them. In the early days the different businesses of a publisher, a bookseller and a bookbinder were often carried on by one man who was called a stationer. He bought books wholesale, sometimes having whole editions specially printed for him, he bound them, and then sold them like an ordinary bookseller. He also probably in England, as was certainly done on the continent, sent round vans full of books to the various provincial towns, timing his arrival as far as possible to coincide with the local fairs.

A considerable number of the books printed abroad for sale in England have no connexion with any particular stationer, but were probably brought over by an agent of the printer and sold in lots to different stationers.

The earliest book printed abroad definitely for sale in England is the edition of the Sarum *Breviary* printed at Cologne about 1475. Of this book nothing is left but a few leaves, and the imprint, if it possessed one, is not known. Only one other book is known printed in the same type, an edition of the *Homilies*, but it, unfortunately, has no imprint, so that we have no clue as to who may have been the printer. I cannot help thinking that perhaps Caxton may have had something to do with having this book printed, commissioning it either on his own account or for some friend in England, for it is unlikely that a printer in so distant a town would have issued such a book on his own account, and the probable date of its printing coincides more or less with Caxton's departure for England.

In 1483 a book was printed at Venice for sale in England, curiously enough another edition of the Sarum *Breviary*. The copy in the Bibliothèque Nationale, the only one known, is a very beautiful book, printed on vellum and quite perfect. There is a rather painful history attached to it. In 1715 this unique book came to the University Library, Cambridge, as part of the library of Bishop Moore which was presented to the University by George I. In the latter half of the eighteenth century it appears to have been purloined along with a great many other rarities by a certain Dr. Combe. It then found its way into the collection of Count Justin MacCarthy, who formed the largest library of books printed on vellum ever brought together by a private collector (he had over 600 of such books), and at his sale early in the present century it was purchased for the Paris library for fifty-one francs. The printer of the book, Reginaldus de Novimagio, does not appear to have had any connexion with England, nor does the imprint mention for whom the book was produced. It is curious that he should have been chosen as the printer of this *Breviary*, for it seems to have been the only liturgical work he issued, and nothing among his other productions has any connexion with England. Of course English people passed through Venice in large quantities as it was the starting point for pilgrims to the Holy Land, and many ecclesiastics of high position went on this journey, so that perhaps one of these travellers, seeing the beautiful work done at Venice, and knowing that no printer at home was equal to the task of producing such a book in a fitting manner, commissioned the printing of the *Breviary*. It is sad to think that so beautiful a book has been lost to England through the dishonesty of a reader in the library. We can only regret that the negotiations between the Duke of Devonshire and the representatives of Count MacCarthy for the purchase of the library *en bloc* fell through, and that the Duke and Lord Spencer, who both bought considerably at the sale, did not secure it, for then at any rate it might have been in England, though not in its proper place.

In the year 1483 some important acts were passed relating to the trading of foreigners in this country. The ninth chapter ends: " Provided always that this act or any parcel thereof, or any other act made, or to be made in this said parliament, shall not extend, or be in prejudice, disturbance, damage, or impediment, to any artificer, or merchant stranger, of what nation or country he be, or shall be of, for bringing into this realm, or selling by retail, or otherwise, any books written or printed, or for inhabiting within this said realm for the same intent, or any scrivener, alluminor, reader or printer of such books, which he hath, or shall have to sell by way of merchandise, or for their dwelling within this said realm, for the exercise of the said occupations; this act or any part thereof notwithstanding".

This act it will be seen, which was not repealed until 1533, gave absolute liberty to foreign printers and stationers to trade and reside in England. That it succeeded in its object of encouraging the immigration of stationers and craftsmen and the importation of books, is clear from the words of the act of 1533: "Whereas by the provision of a Statute made in the firste yere of the reygne of Kynge Richarde the thirde, it was provided in the same acte that all strangers repayryng into this realme might lawfully bring into the saide realme printed and written bokes to sell at their libertie and pleasure. By force of which provision there hath comen into this realme sithen the makynge of the same, a marvellous number of printed bookes and dayly doth. And the cause of the making of the same provision semeth to be, for that there were but few bookes and fewe printers within this realme at that time, whiche could well exercise and occupie the said science and crafte of printynge. Nevertheless, sithen the making of the saide provision, many of this realme being the Kinges naturall subjectes, have given them so diligently to lerne and exercise the saide craft of printing that at this day there be within this realme a great number of connyng and experte in the said science or crafte of printing, as able to exercise the saide crafte in all pointes as any stranger in any other realme or country."

Though the preamble of this act speaks only of printing, it was mainly directed against the foreign bookbinders and stationers. By it it was forbidden to import any foreign printed books ready bound, and no one was to buy from any foreigner residing in England any books except "by engrosse," that is, wholesale. This you will see completely stopped the trade of the foreign binder in the English market, and absolutely did away with the foreign stationer in England. One effect of the act is apparent in the extraordinary number of letters of denisation taken out at that date. In 1582 Christopher Barker wrote: "In the time of King Henry VIII. there were but few printers and those of good credit and competent wealth, at whiche time and before there was another sort of men, that were writers, lymners of bookes and dyverse thinges for the Churche and other uses called stacioners; which have and partly to this day do use to buy their bookes in grosse of the said printers, to bynde them up and sell them in their shops, whereby they well mayntayned their families".

The fifty years then between 1483 and 1533 are the really interesting years in the history of the English book trade, when it was free and unprotected, but though we have a fair amount of information about the latter half of this time, the earlier half is almost destitute of any kind of records. The books of the original company of stationers in London have all disappeared, and we are dependent mostly on incidental references in deeds, in wills or other legal documents.

The year before the act was passed, namely in 1482, we know of two foreign booksellers who had come to London, Henry Frankenberg and Bernard van Stondo, who rented an alley in St. Clement's Lane called St. Mark's Alley. From their names they would appear to have come from the Low Countries, but we know nothing about them or their business beyond the fact that Frankenberg commissioned their fellow-countryman, William de Machlinia, who was printing in London, to print for him an edition of the *Speculum Christiani*, about which I spoke in my last lecture. Their names in the deed and Frankenberg's name in a colophon are the only clues we have to the existence of two probably important booksellers. So also in the very year of the act we find foreign dealers in books trading in Oxford with the resident university stationer.

About 1486 at Louvain, Egidius vander Heerstraten printed an edition of the *Regulae Grammaticales* of Nicolas Perott, which contains a great number of passages in English. These are very curious, and seem to have been translated by one not very conversant with the language. Here is a passage which refers to the fifteenth century substitute for compulsory football: "who someuer of my discipulis goyth awey fryst from the gammyng wt owt my licence i shal smyte his hande wyt a rode. And yf he do that samyn thyng twyss i shall also beet hym wyt a leyshe." In another place, having translated the Latin phrase, "Quintilianus est eloquens sed nihil ad Ciceronem," "Quintilian is a wel spoken man but nothyng to Tully," he adds another and more personal example: "Helia Perott is fayr but nothing to Penelope".

I am not sure whether we ought to consider this book as one printed for the purpose of exportation to England, or whether it was not rather intended for the use of English students at the foreign universities. This is made more probable from the fact that in a few cases we have words translated into Dutch prefaced by "as we say". I have seen it stated that a similar edition was printed by the same printer with explanations in French, but I have not been able to verify the existence of any copy.

About 1486, too, was issued the first edition of the Sarum *Missal*, printed, it is supposed, at Basle by Wenssler, though some doubts have been raised as to whether it was really printed at Basle on account of the appearance of the music type. It is a very handsome folio volume of 278 leaves, printed in a large Gothic type in red and black. The printer has not attempted to print the English portions of the wedding service, but has left blank spaces where they occur, so that they might be written in by hand. The first few editions of the Sarum *Missal* are all similar in this respect, but it is curious that Caxton, who had an edition specially printed for him, should not have supplied the printer with correct copy for these small portions of the service.

In the next few years a few grammatical books were issued, printed as a rule in the Low Countries. In 1486 Gerard Leeu printed the *Vulgaria Terentii*, a series of Latin sentences with translations into English, an edition reprinted from the Oxford one of a year or two earlier. This book is sometimes found printed as a supplement to the *Grammar* by John Anwykyll, and of this *Grammar* there are two foreign editions, one printed by Paffroed at Deventer in 1489, and another rather later by Henry Quentell at Cologne. The *Grammar* does not contain an author's name, but in the prefatory verses written by Petrus Carmelianus he is referred to as Joannes. There are also verses written to William Waynflete, Bishop of Winchester and founder of Magdalen College, Oxford, congratulating him on having persuaded this Joannes to edit the *Grammar*. The book is supposed to have been intended for the use of the Magdalen College School, in which the two grammarians John Anwykyll and John Stanbridge were masters, and is supposed to have been the work of Anwykyll. The two earliest editions were printed at Oxford, but by 1489 the Oxford Press had stopped work and the two succeeding editions were printed abroad.

The two works attributed to Joannes de Garlandia, the *Liber Equivocorum* and *Liber Synonymorum*, were also printed in the Low Countries, the first at Deventer by Paffroed, the second at Antwerp by Thierry Martens in 1493. The *Liber Synonymorum* has the commentary of Galfridus Anglicus. A copy of this book sold in the Ratcliffe sale in the last century was described as having been printed at Antwerp in 1492, but this must have been, I suppose, a misprint for 1493.

Three more books printed in the Low Countries I ought to mention before turning to France. One is an edition of Clement Maydeston's *Directorium Sacerdotum*, printed by Gerard Leeu in 1488, of which there is a copy in the University Library.

Another is an edition of the Sarum *Horae*, also printed by Leeu, which I am afraid has to be spoken of at present as a lost book. The only fragment known, an unused half sheet containing eight leaves, had been used to line the binding of a copy of the *Scriptores rei rusticae* printed at Reggio in 1496, in Brasenose College Library; Bradshaw saw the fragment and took down a description of it, but on its return to Oxford it was mislaid and is not to be found.

The third book is another edition of the Sarum *Breviary*, printed at Louvain in 1499 by Thierry Martens. The only copy known is in the Musée Plantin at Antwerp. Leaving the Low Countries for a time we will turn to France.

The *Missal* printed for Caxton in 1487 I have already

described in an earlier lecture, so I can pass on to the edition which succeeded it, that printed by Martin Morin, the celebrated printer of Rouen in 1492. This Morin was by far the most important of the Norman stationers and printers, and he appears to have excelled in the printing of service books, for he was employed by printers and publishers from all parts to print the service books for the special use of the towns where they resided.

For England he printed altogether six service books in the fifteenth century. Three *Missals*, two *Breviaries*, and a *Liber Festivalis*, and of these the *Missal* of 1492 is the earliest. The two copies known of this book, both slightly imperfect, are in the British Museum and the Bodleian. It contains, like the earlier edition printed for Caxton, two full-page engravings before the Canon of the Mass, not one only as is more generally the case.

The two later *Missals* which he issued, one without date but about 1495 and another dated 1497, appear to have been mixed up by all writers. The undated edition appears the rarest, for the only copy which I have noted is in the British Museum. Of the dated edition I have notes of five, one at Windsor in the Queen's library, one in St. Catherine's College, one at Chatsworth, one in the Aberdeen University Library, and the fifth at Kinnaird Castle. I owe my knowledge of the existence of this last copy to almost the last book in which one would seek for bibliographical information, the current edition of *Who's Who*. Both editions are very handsome books, remarkable for their fine titles and initial letters.

Of the two *Breviaries* which Morin printed the earliest is dated 1496, and the only copy known is in the University Library at Edinburgh, to which it was bequeathed in 1577 by Clement Litill, who left a number of valuable books to that library of which he was practically the founder. It is a magnificent folio volume of 437 leaves, and contains a fairly full imprint, which after a deal of very grandiloquent language tells us that the book was printed at the cost of Jean Richard " by the industry of that man skilled in printing Mr. Martin Morin a not unworthy citizen of that great city Rouen". Morin's colophons I may note rarely err on the side of modesty. The Jean Richard mentioned was a stationer of Rouen, and one who appears to have had considerable dealings with England. I do not think he was a printer as is often stated, and he describes himself as a dealer in books, not a printer, using sometimes the word merchant of books and sometimes the word stationer.

It was for him that Morin printed in 1499 an edition of Mirk's *Liber Festivalis* and *Quattuor Sermones*, a copy of which is in the Sandars collection in the University Library. For him also, in 1500, a Sarum *Manual* was printed by Petrus Olivier and Joannes de Lorraine, of which there is a copy in the Bodleian, and during the early years of the sixteenth century a considerable number of service books for the English market were printed at his expense.

The names of a number of early stationers who probably traded between Rouen and England are to be found in the imprints of the early Sarum *Missals*, for as the printing of them entailed a good deal of expense a number of booksellers would combine to pay for the edition. Rouen seems to have been, amongst all the towns of France, the most connected with England as regards the book trade. It was there many of our printers, as well as the first Scottish printers, learned their art or obtained their materials, while stationers from that town crossed over and sold their books in this country.

We know that Ingelbert Haghe, the publisher of the Hereford *Breviary* of 1505, came over himself and sold books at Hereford and in the country round. On the flyleaf of a Bible formerly in the library of Gloucester Cathedral is a Latin inscription which runs: "I gave to the Hereford bookseller called Ingelbert for this and the six other volumes of the bible 43 shillings and fourpence, which I bought at Ludlow the year of our Lord's incarnation 1510, about the day of the Lichfield fair ". Whether the Bible is still in the Gloucester Cathedral Library I do not know, but the fly-leaves which once belonged to it are in a bundle of scraps in the Bodleian.

Another Rouen printer issued in 1495 an edition of the *Liber Festivalis*. His name was James Ravynell, and this is the only book that he is known to have printed. It is an exact copy of the edition printed by W. de Worde in 1493 and '94, and the type used in it has a very clean and new appearance. At the end is a device with the initials P. R., which looks as though it might have been made for another member of the family, though we know of no other printer of the name. The fact that he uses the English form of the Christian name in the imprint, " By me, James Ravynell," looks as if he was an Englishman who had migrated to Rouen.

The device consists of the initials P. R. on a shield suspended by a belt from a tree and supported by two muzzled bears. Below the shield two birds hold up a wreath. Round the whole runs the text: " Junior fui etenim senui et non vidi justum derelictum nec semen ejus querens panem". The name Ravynell is a curious one, and may be a corrupted spelling of a commoner name.

Another mysterious book, which from its type may very well have been printed at Rouen, is an edition of the little grammar called *Parvula*. It consists only of four leaves, and the only copy known is at Manchester. The book ends: " Here endeth a treatise called parvula, for the instruction of children. Emprentyd by me Nicole Marcant." In the exasperating way common to some printers both the date and place of printing are omitted. As to the date I am inclined to put it before 1500, but the place is more difficult to settle. Nicole Marcant is an unknown printer, but may very well be a member of one of the numerous families of

Marchand or Mercator, for there were several printers of that name, though none so far as I know named Nicholas.

If we except the *Missal* printed for Caxton in 1487 it was not until 1494 that the Paris printers began to work for the English market, and the books they produced were almost all liturgical. The only exceptions are three editions of grammatical works ascribed to Joannes de Garlandia, two of the *Liber Equivocorum* and one of the *Liber Synonymorum*, the first two printed by Baligault and the last by Hopyl.

The first liturgical book was an edition of the Sarum *Breviary*, printed in 1494 by Pierre Levet. For a long time only one copy was known, that in the library at Trinity College, Dublin, but not long ago the University Library was fortunate enough to secure a second example, a very beautiful copy in its old binding.

In one thing the Paris printers excelled all others, and that was in the production of books of hours. These were turned out in the last few years of the century by hundreds of thousands, and though they are now of very common occurrence and very often of little interest, they are still much sought after by certain classes of collectors, especially those who like what they call pretty books. Of course, when these books were printed for the use of out of the way places they have often great liturgical interest, and being printed no doubt in small quantities are very rare. The English service books having been relentlessly destroyed at the Reformation are very rare indeed. Altogether in the fifteenth century twenty-five editions of the Sarum *Hours* were printed, fourteen in England, one at Antwerp, and ten in Paris, but nine English editions were printed before one was issued at Paris, so that these latter when once they got a footing in England easily defied competition. The changes in the text of these books during the last ten years of the century are very curious and interesting. The

Horae was not a service book proper, but a manual of private devotion, and so long as it contained certain fixed and definite parts additional prayers could be added at will. Consequently the editions vary greatly, and each publisher seems to have aimed at inserting new and popular prayers, and by 1500 the book had increased to almost double the bulk of its forerunner of ten years earlier.

In speaking of these books there is one point on which a word of warning may be said. And that is about dating editions which have no date in the imprint. All such are usually put down to 1488, which is the first date printed in the calendar of movable feasts. As this calendar was made out for a nineteen year cycle running on to 1508 it was naturally not reprinted for many years, and therefore is no test in dating the printing of the book. The nine editions printed at Paris are the work of about five printers, of whom the most important was Felix Baligault.

The study of these French books of hours is not an easy one, as there is so much confusion between printers and publishers. In some cases I am afraid the publishers used the words "printed by" in a quite unwarrantable manner, and claimed to have produced books which they had done nothing more than pay for. Then again quite half the ones produced for sale in England are without any imprint, so that we are left to conjecture who was the printer from the type or cuts used in the books. To further bewilder us sets of cuts passed from printer to printer, and are very untrustworthy guides in assigning books. If one printer issued a *Horae* with a fine set of cuts they were promptly copied by his rivals, who in their turn sold their old sets to less wealthy printers, in fact some sets of cuts change hands almost every year.

These books are all got up in the same style, the text surrounded on every page by deep borders containing figures of saints and martyrs or pictures from the dance of death.

One unique edition, printed by Jean Poitevin about 1498, was picked up lately in Ireland and bought by the Trinity College librarian for a small sum.

A service book of great interest is the first edition of the Sarum *Manual*, of which the only known copy is in the library at Caius. It bears on its first leaf a Latin inscription stating that it was given to the College of the Annunciation of the Blessed Mary at Cambridge by Humphrey de la Poole, son of the Duke of Suffolk, for the use of the college, in September, 1498. The book is a folio of 164 leaves, beautifully printed in red and black by Berthold Rembolt of Paris. It has no date, but the Greek in the printer's device reads ΧΕΡΕΘΗΚΙ, and must therefore be after 1496 when it read ΧΕΡΕΘΙΚΗ, and as the book was presented in 1498 we may fairly safely fix the date of printing about the beginning of 1498. Unfortunately, the last leaf is missing which may have contained an imprint giving the exact date and stating for whom the book was printed.

The last service book to be noticed is a Sarum *Missal* printed by Jean du Pré at Paris in 1500. Unfortunately all the copies of this book are imperfect.

All these service books though most interesting liturgically are almost the most uninteresting class of book to the bibliographer. They were issued by well-known printers, and are hardly different from the great mass of foreign service books. From them early in the sixteenth century, however, we derive a good deal of information about the stationers, especially as regards the provincial presses; for in the case of a town like York hardly anything seems to have been printed beyond liturgical books.

So far the books we have been speaking of have been for the most part in Latin, with some sentences here and there in English, printed, of course, for the English market, but not of much interest from the point of view of literature. But we now come to another small group of

English books, printed entirely in English, of very much greater interest.

In 1492 and 1493, when, just after the death of Caxton, the English press was almost at a standstill, Gerard Leeu of Antwerp printed four English books of considerable interest. Three of them were reprints of books already printed by Caxton, Lefevre's *Life of Jason*, the *History of Paris and Vienne*, and the *Chronicles of England*. The fourth book was the *Dialogue or Communing between the Wise King Solomon and Marcolphus*. Of this there does not seem to have been any other English edition, though many Latin ones were printed in the fifteenth century, and it is possible though hardly probable that Caxton might have printed an edition which has entirely disappeared.

Lefevre's *History of Jason* is a small folio of ninety-eight leaves, illustrated with a number of half-page cuts clearly made to illustrate the book in which they first appear. They were used in several editions of the *Jason* in different languages, the earliest in Dutch having been printed by Bellaert at Haarlem about 1485. There are copies of the English edition at Trinity College, Dublin, and in the library at Chatsworth, and a third copy, slightly imperfect, is in the University Library.

The *History of Paris and Vienne*, which was printed exactly three weeks after the *History of Jason*, is a still rarer book, only one copy being known, which is in the library at Trinity College, Dublin. It, like the *Jason*, is illustrated with a series of half-page wood engravings, which Mr. Conway, in his *History of the Woodcutters of the Netherlands*, conjectures to have been originally used in an edition printed by Bellaert at Haarlem, which has now entirely disappeared, and then to have passed from his possession into the hands of Gerard Leeu. It is a small folio of forty leaves, and the copy at Dublin is bound up with the *Jason* and the *Chronicles*.

LECTURE III.

The next book to be noticed, the *Dialogue or Communyng between the Wise King Solomon and Marcolphus*, is very interesting, being the only English edition of this version of a widespread and popular story. It tells how Solomon, seated on his throne, is confronted by Marcolphus, a misshapen rustic who answers with a certain coarse wit the questions put to him by the king. Later on the king visits Marcolphus, who in his turn comes to reside at court, but his behaviour there is so insolent that the king can hardly put up with it. After a series of escapades Marcolphus is banished from the court, and finally sentenced to be hanged. He is allowed as a favour to choose his own tree, and consequently he wanders with his guards through the Vale of Josaphath to Jericho, over Jordan, through Arabia and the wilderness to the Red Sea, but "never more could Marcolf find a tree that he wold choose to hang on". The curious result of this is that he went home and lived happily ever afterwards.

The book itself has only one illustration, which is used twice, on the recto and verso of the title-page, representing Marcolphus and his wife Polycana standing before Solomon, who is seated upon his throne. This cut found its way over to England, and was used by several successive printers for editions of *Howleglas*.

The only copy known of *Solomon and Marcolphus* is in the Bodleian, and was in a volume of tracts bequeathed with his library by Thomas Tanner, Bishop of St. Asaph. The volume contained originally five separate pieces. Two by Wynkyn de Worde, the *Three Kings of Coleyne* and the *Meditations of St. Bernard*, two by Caxton, the *Governayle of Health* and the *Ars morendi*, and the *Solomon and Marcolphus*. I am sorry to say that the two Caxtons have been cut out of the volume and bound separately.

The last of the four books to be noticed is the edition of the *Chronicles of England*. While the *Chronicles* were being printed Gerard Leeu died, or perhaps it would be more correct to say was murdered. One of his workmen named Henric van Symmen, who was also a type engraver, struck work and determined to set up in business on his own account. This led to a quarrel, and blows succeeded words. The workman, it appears, in the course of the quarrel struck Leeu a blow on the head, and this proved so serious that he lay very ill for three days and then died. The workman was promptly secured and brought up for trial for the killing of his master, but it was probably considered that he had received a certain amount of aggravation, and his punishment took the form of a fine. He was sentenced to pay into the Duke of Burgundy's exchequer the sum of forty guelden. Gerard Leeu seems to have been a good master and a kindly man if we may judge from the colophon put to the *Chronicles*: "Enprentyd In the Duchye of Braband in the towne of Andewarpe In the yere of our lord M.cccc.xciii. By maister Gerard de Leew a man of grete wysedom in all maner of kunnyng: whych nowe is come from lyfe unto the deth, which is grete harme for many a poure man. On whos sowle god almyghty for hys hygh grace haue mercy. Amen."

The book contains no illustrations beyond a woodcut of the arms of England on the title-page.

Leeu seems to have intended to print more English books, for the type in which all but the *Chronicles* are printed was a special fount cut in imitation of English type, with a curious lower case d for use when that letter occurred at the end of a word. His death, however, so soon after the cutting of the type, put an end to all such plans. The custom, however, of printing English books at Antwerp revived at the very beginning of the sixteenth century, for Adrian van Berghen printed an edition of Holt's *Lac Puerorum*, and John of Doesborch issued a whole series of English popular books, some of them remarkably curious.

Among the stationers who came to England from abroad the most important was certainly Frederick Egmont. He was probably a Frenchman, but his printing was mainly done in Venice, and he seems to have been the agent of the Venetian printer Johannes Hertzog de Landoia. From this Venetian press came a large number of service books for English use, editions of the *Breviary* and *Missal*. The Sarum *Horae* on the other hand was never printed at Venice, but mainly at Paris.

Egmont during his earliest years as a stationer was connected with no press except that of Hertzog, and we do not know of any books by this printer produced for any other English stationer, so that as regards liturgical books for English use known to us now only from fragments, we are justified, I think, in attributing to Egmont as stationer such as we can determine from their type to have been printed by Hertzog.

The first book in which his name occurs is an edition of the *Breviary* according to the use of York, of which the only known copy is in the Bodleian, having been originally in the great liturgical collection of Richard Gough. It is a small thick octavo of 462 pages, and was issued in May, 1493. Two if not three editions of the Sarum *Breviary* in octavo were printed about this same time, but we know of their existence only from fragments discovered in bindings. Fragments of one edition are in a binding in the library of St. John's College, of another in a binding at Lambeth, while some leaves of probably a third edition are in the library of Corpus Christi College, Oxford.

In 1494 Egmont had commissioned Hertzog to print for him two editions of the Sarum *Missal*, one in folio, the other in octavo. The folio edition is of great rarity, but there is a beautiful though slightly imperfect copy in the Sandars collection in the University Library. The title-page is wanting and also the leaf containing the engraving of the Crucifixion which should precede the Canon of the Mass. In the imprint we are told that the book was finished on the 1st of September, 1494, by John Hertzog de Landoia for Fredericus de Egmont and Gerardus Barrevelt. This Gerardus Barrevelt was clearly a partner of Egmont's, as their initials occur together in the device on the title-page. This device is remarkable for the delicacy of its execution. It consists of a circle divided by a perpendicular line produced beyond the top of the circle, the projection being crossed by two bars. In the left-hand half of the circle are the initials and mark of Egmont, in the right those of Barrevelt. The whole is enclosed in a square frame, and the background contains sprays of leaves. It so resembles in style and appearance the mark used by the printer John Hertzog that we may be pretty certain it was cut under his supervision at Venice.

The octavo *Missal* of 1494, a much commoner book than the last, was issued in December, 1494. On the last leaf is Hertzog's mark and the words, " Fredericus egmont me fieri fecit ". There is no mention of Barrevelt, and the double device does not occur in the book, which makes it appear as though this edition was printed for Egmont alone. Both these editions of the *Missal* contain the most exquisitely designed woodcut initials, the most graceful to be found in any early book.

In the Bodleian there is a copy of the " Pars estivalis " of the Sarum *Breviary* printed at Venice in 1495, which contains again the device of Egmont and Barrevelt, though the imprint mentions Egmont's name only. After 1495 we hear nothing more of Egmont until 1499, when he seems to have got rid of his former partner Barrevelt and joined with a man named Peter post pacha, and these two commissioned Pynson to print them an edition of the *Promptorium Puerorum*. After 1499 Egmont disappeared for a long time, we know of him working as a bookbinder, and it is probable that he stayed on for some time in England, but when he does reappear it is in Paris where he had some books printed for him about 1517-1520.

It is very disappointing that we have practically no information about Frederick Egmont, for it is clear from the number of books that he had printed for him in Venice that he must have been a stationer of very considerable importance. The colophons of his books give, beyond his mere name, no information whatever about him: we do not even know in what part of London or under what sign he lived. The stationers seem always to have settled in St. Paul's Churchyard, and I cannot help thinking that part of that district may have been "in the liberties," as it was called, of some church. Though the act of Richard allowed foreigners to come over and trade, yet I do not suppose his act could override the rights of the trade guilds. It certainly did not in York, for there a stationer must be a freeman by right or by purchase before he could carry on certain businesses, that of a stationer amongst the number, within the city. There were, however, certain liberties where an alien could live and trade; and we find at York that their earliest stationer, Gerard Wanseford, does not appear in the city register. Having taken up his abode within the liberty of St. Peter he was privileged to carry on business there without being a freeman of the city.

In the same way in London, I suppose, the various trades had their rights and could prevent foreigners from competing, except they resided within the liberties. Of course there was a Stationers' Company in London in the fifteenth century, though unfortunately most of the records relating to it have disappeared, and it would protect its own members. We see in the early bindings how ostentatiously the binders who were freemen decorated their bindings with the arms of London, and there is no doubt that as far as trading in the city was concerned the foreigner was considerably handicapped in comparison with the freeman.

THE STATIONERS. 79

We know from the few early documents remaining that the London Company of Stationers was a powerful and important body, and the members of it must certainly have enjoyed certain privileges.

Nicholas Lecomte was another stationer who appears to have been settled in England by 1494, in which year, so far as I know, his first dated book appears. M. Madden, a French writer on early printing, in the fifth volume of his *Lettres d'un Bibliographe*, speaks of Hopyl having printed a book for Lecomte in 1493. Several times in writing to him I asked for some information about this book, its whereabouts or its name even, but though he sent always voluminous replies to my letters, he never would touch on this particular point. I think, therefore, we may consider that this 1493 book never existed, and take the 1494 book as the first. This was an edition of the *Liber Synonymorum*, printed by Hopyl, of which there are copies in the University Library, the British Museum, and the Bodleian.

In the imprint Lecomte is described as living in London by St. Paul's Churchyard at the Sign of St. Nicholas. His device depicts St. Nicholas restoring to life the three children who had been killed and pickled, a favourite subject of the early bookbinders.

I think it is worth noting here, that so far as I can discover the sign of a house was not in any way permanent, but could apparently be changed at will. I noticed this in reading through a catalogue or *précis* of some thousands of deeds relating to property in London at this time and a little earlier. We find endless notices of houses with changed signs, "the tenement now called the Rose, formerly the Lion," the "house called the Bull, formerly called the Rose," and so on. Naturally, if a house got celebrated for any reason it would be politic to keep the sign, but there seems to have been no compulsion to do so.

In 1495 an edition of Mirk's *Liber Festivalis* and *Quattuor*

Sermones was printed by Hopyl for Lecomte. This contains Lecomte's device at the end of the *Liber Festivalis* and a curious device at the end of the *Quattuor Sermones*, used sometimes by Hopyl, but which does not bear on its face any appearance of having been made for him.

At the time when this book was printed Hopyl had in his office as press corrector an Edinburgh man called David Lauxius, the earliest Scotchman we know of employed in a printing office. He afterwards became a schoolmaster at Arras, and appears to have been a man of considerable ability, and a friend of the celebrated Parisian printer and editor, Badius Ascencius, who addresses to him some of the prefatory letters in his grammars. What Scotch name is represented by the Latin Lauxius no one has yet been able to determine.

The last book printed for Lecomte was printed at Paris by Jean Jehannot, and is an edition of the Sarum *Horae*. It is a book of very great rarity, but there are two copies in Cambridge, one in Trinity College, and the other in the Sandars collection in the University Library, the latter containing a small supplement not found in the other copies, and which was not originally intended to form part of the book, since the prayers in it are not referred to in the list of contents. The imprint is curious, it states that the edition has been revised and corrected in the celebrated University of Paris, and printed for Nicolas Lecomte of that University, settled for the time being in England as a merchant of books. I do not know whether this means merely that he was educated at the University or whether he was one of the privileged stationers attached to it, though in the latter case he would hardly have come to settle in England. Like Frederick Egmont, Lecomte was also a bookbinder.

Before the end of the century another stationer was settled in England whose name we know, John Boudins.

We know of only one book printed for him, an edition of the *Expositio Hymnorum et Sequentiarum* of Salisbury use, which was printed at the beginning of 1502 by Bocard of Paris. Boudins was probably then an old man, for his will is dated the 11th of October, 1501, and it was proved on the 30th of March, 1503. He lived in the parish of St. Clement's, Eastcheap, and was apparently a naturalised Fleming, and an immigrant from Antwerp.

A great difficulty in the way of tracing these stationers, especially those from the Low Countries, is the very sparing use they made of their proper surnames. In legal documents such as wills or letters of denizåtion the formal name would be given, whereas in ordinary parlance and in the imprints of books they would be spoken of by a kind of nickname taken from the town from which they came, like William de Machlinia, Wynkyn de Worde, and so on. So that we should probably find, if we had more information on the subject, that in many cases two men who are treated as different may turn out to be only one man under two names. The number of stationers that must have existed at this time in England was probably very large, and it is sad to think that our information on the subject is so meagre. Of course unless the stationer was wealthy enough or in a good way of business he would not be able to commission whole editions of books from a foreign printer, and therefore he would not have his name in the imprint. Then again the greater part of a stationer's stock would consist of foreign books which were not essentially printed for England. For information of this class we can only look to MS. sources, accounts kept by the bookseller, lists of imported books, and so on.

There exists, for instance, a list of books for sale at Oxford in 1483 by Thomas Hunte, which has been edited by Mr. Madan in the Oxford Historical Society publications. At the head of the list is the following sentence in Latin:

"Here follows the inventory of the books which I, Thomas Hunte, stationer of the University of Oxford, have received from Master Peter Actor and John of Aix-la-Chapelle to sell, with the price of each book, and I promise faithfully to return the books or the money according to the price written below as it appears in the following list". The two men mentioned were no doubt travelling stationers, supplying so much stock to the bookseller on a system of sale or return.

A document such as the *Day-Book of John Dorne*, the journal or account-book of an Oxford bookseller in 1520, which was edited by Mr. Madan for the Oxford Historical Society, and about which Henry Bradshaw wrote his half-century of notes, the last piece of work which he finished, is a find of the utmost importance in our subject, and it is perhaps not too much to expect that more documents of this kind may be forthcoming. In the account book we notice that after the 21st of May up to the 3rd of August there is an entire blank, and Dorne begins his account-book again "post recessum meum de ultra mare". I think we should be safe in concluding that these months were spent abroad on business and in the purchase of books.

Sometimes such information is found amongst the waste leaves used to make boards for bindings. The University librarian read a note before the Antiquarian Society here giving an account of a letter on business matters written from a foreign printer to John Siberch, the first printer in Cambridge, which was found amongst other waste matter used to make the boards of a binding now in Westminster Abbey Library, and letters of bookbinders have been found in the same way.

We have not, unfortunately, any book however meagre on this subject which might serve as a basis on which to build up information. Isolated facts turn up occasionally here or there, but there being no regular place for us to put them they drop out of sight again. And it is only when we have collected a number of these facts and begin to find the links that piece them together that we can arrive at any definite knowledge of the subject.

I do not suppose we may expect to find much new information from books themselves, though from MS. sources a good deal may yet be discovered. Within the last year or two many documents relating to stationers and printers of the early sixteenth century have been found at the Rolls Office, and there must be many more still to be found there; besides, the documents in the Rolls Office are only a part of our great collections.

However, as I said before, what we most want is an account as full as possible of the booksellers and stationers up to 1535, giving us all the information that has yet been discovered, to serve as a groundwork for what may be found in the future.

LECTURE IV.

THE BOOKBINDERS.

From the very earliest times the bookbindings produced in England were remarkable for their beauty and richness. The finest were of gold, ornamented with gems, but their value has led to their destruction, and I do not think that there is any early binding of this class now in existence. Leather was very soon recognised as a suitable material for book covers, being easily worked and capable of receiving a considerable amount of ornament. The earliest leather binding known is on a beautiful little manuscript of St. John's Gospel, taken from the tomb of St. Cuthbert, and now preserved in the library of Stonyhurst College. It is of red leather, and the centre of the side is ornamented with a raised ornament of Celtic design, while above and below are small panels filled with interlaced lines, executed apparently with a pointed tool and coloured yellow. This binding is generally considered to be of the tenth century, though there are some reasons for thinking that it may have been executed later, but if this is so the present binding must have been copied from an earlier one.

Excellent as the early work had been, that of the twelfth and thirteenth centuries is unsurpassed. The leather bindings executed at Durham for Bishop Pudsey between 1153 and 1195 are marvellous both for their detail and for their general effect. It was the custom of binders of this period to build up a bold and effective pattern covering the whole side of the book by means of a large number of dies, beautifully engraved with different designs. On the four volumes of Bishop Pudsey's Bible, now in the Cathedral Library at Durham, no less than fifty-one different dies are used, and when we remember that Bishop Pudsey was one of the great builders of the cathedral, it is not surprising that the ornamentation on the dies used in these bindings should resemble the carved work in the cathedral. There are in the Cathedral Library seven of these early bindings, and, unfortunately, they have suffered a considerable amount of mutilation at a not very remote date, for visitors on payment of a small gratuity to the person who looked after the library were allowed to cut out with a penknife one of the stamps to keep as a curiosity. A few more Durham bindings, easily recognised by the dies, are scattered in different libraries in London and in France.

At Winchester, too, and London very beautiful work of the same class was produced, the circular form of decoration being very much made use of. Perhaps the finest piece of Winchester work now in existence is the binding of the *Winchester Domesday Book* in the library of the Society of Antiquaries, of which a facsimile was published in the illustrated catalogue of the exhibition of bookbindings at the Burlington Fine Arts Club. Some very fine work, too, probably executed at Winchester, is to be found on some manuscripts in the library of the Faculty of Medicine at Montpellier, executed before 1146 for Henry, son of Louis VII. of France.

The metal dies with which these bindings were stamped were practically indestructible, but it is curious to notice that they hardly ever appear to have been used after the twelfth and early thirteenth centuries. I only know of one case to the contrary. In Westminster Abbey Library is a copy of the *Epistolae* of Ficinus, printed in 1495, which has its covers ornamented with early Winchester stamps.

In all these early bindings one is especially struck with the extraordinary taste and balance in the decoration. The dies themselves are beautiful, and the pattern in which they are built up is also beautiful, and yet neither are unduly emphasised. In later bindings the die became smaller and less finely cut. It was not intended to be decorative in itself, but only to help to build up patterns, and the bindings in consequence lose much of their interest.

Oxford, I believe, is generally credited with clinging somewhat strongly to old traditions, and certainly its bookbinders did so in the fifteenth century. From the earliest times bookbinding had been considerably practised there and continued without a break, and no doubt that is why the old styles lingered for so long. The bindings produced there towards the end of the century form the connecting link between the old styles and the new. They represent the last survival of the early English school of work, that very distinctive English style which depended so much on the disposal of dies into large circles, or parallelograms one inside the other, such as we find in the Winchester and Durham bindings of the twelfth or thirteenth centuries. That this circular work was not the haphazard freak of a single binder we can see from the fact that several of the dies are wider at the top than at the bottom, so that when placed together side by side they would naturally work round to a circular form, like the stones forming the arch of a bridge. These dies are in many cases foreign in design and may have been introduced by Rood, the first printer, but the style of binding is essentially English. Some bindings of a rather similar appearance, though never with any circular ornament, were produced in the Low Countries. On nearly all Oxford bindings will be found little groups of three small circles, so small that they might have been done with the end of a watch-key, and arranged in a triangle. This ornament I have never seen on any but Oxford work. One habit connects the Oxford binders with those of the Low Countries, and that is their habit of always when possible lining the boards of the binding with leaves of vellum rather than paper. All the other English binders used paper generally for this purpose. It is owing to this custom of using vellum that many copies of *Indulgences* issued by the early printers have been preserved, for, as they were only printed on one side, the binder could paste them down with the printing side next the boards and the clean side outwards. An Oxford binding with an inscription stating that it was bound in "Catte Strete" in 1467 was formerly in the British Museum: the manuscript which it covered has been rebound and the old binding has disappeared.

Caxton, as one would naturally expect, followed the style of binding which he had become used to during his residence at Bruges, though it is interesting to notice that one at least of his dies was directly copied from early London work and applied in the same manner. His general method of covering the side of his binding was to make a large centre panel contained by a framework of dies or lines running about an inch from the edge of the side and intersecting each other at the corners as in the frame known as an Oxford frame. The large panel thus produced on the side was divided into lozenge-shaped compartments by diagonal lines running both ways from the frame, and in each of these compartments a die was stamped. The die most commonly found on his bindings is a square one with some fabulous winged monster engraved upon it, and this very die we find later in the hands of a stationer in London named Jacobi. The broad frame was often made up by repetitions of a triangular stamp, pointing alternately right and left, and containing the figure of a dragon. This stamp is interesting, not only because the use of a triangular stamp was very uncommon, but because it was an exact copy of one used by a London binder about the end of the twelfth century. Very few of Caxton's own books in their original binding have come down to our time, but there is a copy of the second edition of the

Liber Festivalis in the British Museum which was clearly bound by him, and the *Boethius* which was found in the Grammar School at St. Alban's was also in its original cover. The *Royal Book* in the Bedfordshire General Library is in an absolutely similar binding to the *Liber Festivalis* in the British Museum, ornamented with the same die, and with the boards lined with two waste copies of an *Indulgence*. Caxton's bindings were invariably of leather, he never used vellum as many writers have stated. Blades, who was amongst the number, refers to a vellum-bound Caxton in the Bodleian, and states that it is the original binding; but had he examined the book more carefully he would have found that it was made up from two copies, and that the binding therefore could not well be original. Indeed the particular binding was put on in the seventeenth century while the book belonged to Selden. Selden's bindings had good need to be flexible, for one of his customs did not tend to improve bindings. He used to buy his spectacles, like the youth in the *Vicar of Wakefield*, by the gross, and whenever he stopped reading a book he put in the pair he happened to be using to mark the place. It was quite a common thing, soon after his library came to the Bodleian, for spectacles to drop out of the books as they were taken incautiously from the shelves.

Of course the number of bindings which can with certainty be ascribed to Caxton is necessarily small, we can in the first place take only those on books printed by him, and which contain distinct evidence from the fragments used in the binding that they came from his workshop. By means of the stamps used on these we can identify others which have no other materials for identification. Caxton used sometimes wooden boards in his bindings and sometimes waste leaves of printed matter pasted together. These pads of old printing frequently yield most valuable prizes. The copy of Caxton's *Boethius*, found by Blades in the library of the St. Alban's Grammar School, had its boards made of printed matter, which, when carefully taken to pieces, were found to be made of fifty-six half-sheets of paper, forming portions of thirteen books printed by Caxton, three of which were quite unknown.

Caxton's binding stamps passed with his printing material to his successor, Wynkyn de Worde. I found in a college library at Oxford a book with these stamps, evidently bound by De Worde, and the boards were lined with waste leaves of three books printed by him, one being unknown, and one by Caxton. De Worde's bindings are the least easily identified of any in the fifteenth century, for beyond these few dies of Caxton's there are none that can definitely be ascribed to him, and even the various bindings that might be ascribed to him from the fragments found in them seem to vary so much in style and decoration that it seems impossible that they could have all come from one shop. Perhaps he had really no binding establishment of his own, but got such work as he required done by others.

Wynkyn de Worde, as we learn from his will, employed several binders. He left bequests to Alard, bookbinder, his servant, and to Nowel, the bookbinder in Shoe Lane. James Gaver, who was one of his executors, was one of the large family of Gavere, binders in the Low Countries, and though, when he took out letters of denization on his own account in 1535 he is described as a stationer, no doubt he was also a bookbinder. The square stamp with a dragon, which had belonged to Caxton and which must have passed to De Worde, found its way early in the sixteenth century into the hands of another stationer, Henry Jacobi.

The bindings which were produced by Lettou and Machlinia, so far as we are able to identify them, are very plain. The sides are divided by diagonal lines into diamond-shaped compartments, and in each is stamped a small and uninteresting die. The Latin Bible in Jesus College Library, which has every quire lined with slips of vellum, portions of two cut-up copies of Lettou's *Indulgence*, and presumably bound by him, has its binding ornamented with diagonal lines within a frame formed of square dies containing the figure of a fabulous animal. In the diamond-shaped compartments formed by the diagonal lines is a small impressed cinquefoil. Another Lettou binding, on the copy of the *Wallensis* printed by him in 1481 in the Bodleian, is ornamented simply with diagonal lines, but has no small stamps.

There is another English binder of this time whose name we do not know, who produced some very good work. Bradshaw, I think, considered that he worked at Norwich. There are a number of his books in Cambridge libraries, and he used very often a red-coloured leather, which is common in Cambridge bindings. His dies are Low Country in type, and very much resemble those used at Oxford, but his work can be recognised by one peculiarity. He always ornamented the ends of the bands, the bands being those ridges on the back where the leather covers the string or cord on which the quires are stitched. Where these bands ended on the sides he printed a kind of ornament of leaves. He also, like the Oxford binders, almost always lined his boards with vellum.

Pynson's earliest bindings are as a rule very plain. Like the other binders of the time he ruled diagonal lines across the sides of his books, and put a small die in each division. Sometimes he did not even use a die, but contented himself with plain lines, as, for instance, on the copy of his first dated book of 1492 at Appleby. His bindings, like Machlinia's, are very plain, and the dies used are small and poor.

Another binder, perhaps at St. Alban's, produced bindings not unlike Pynson's, but he is identified by a small circular die which he used, which has on it the figure of a bird.

THE BOOKBINDERS. 91

Another binder whose initials were G. W., but whose name we do not know, produced a large number of bindings in the fifteenth century. It is from his bindings that all the fragments of Machlinia's *Horae ad usum Sarum* have been recovered, for he seems to have used up a copy for lining his boards, and luckily several books bound about that time have been preserved. Bradshaw found a curious case of the preservation of two volumes bound in the same workshop about the same time. In the library of St. John's is a copy of a book printed at Nuremberg in 1505, which has in its cover some leaves of early Oxford printing. In the library at Corpus is an exactly similar binding on a book printed at Lyons in 1511, which also contains some early Oxford leaves. Now it is clear that the same man must have bound these books about the same time, because we find in both, along with the refuse Oxford leaves, some leaves from one and the same vellum manuscript.

There is one English binder, who worked before the end of the fifteenth century, who is distinctly worthy of special mention on account of the striking originality of his method of decoration and designs. His name, unfortunately, we do not know, but as one of his most frequently used dies represents a balance or pair of scales it has been conjectured that this may be a rebus on his name, such as many binders used, and that he was called "Scales". Two volumes executed by this binder are known, which were done for a certain William Langton, and the centre panel is ornamented with a rebus on the name Langton, the letters Lang over a barrel or tun, while the rest of the side is filled up with little stamps. This Langton may perhaps be identified with the William Langton who was a prebendary of Lincoln and afterwards of York at the end of the fifteenth century. Another even more curious binding by this same man is in the library of Corpus Christi College, Cambridge. He has disposed his dies so as to form a large heraldic shield, covering the whole side of a folio volume, a style of adornment quite unique so far as I am aware, and as an ornament extremely effective, though I am afraid the heraldry is hardly sufficiently accurate to enable us to determine for whom the volume was bound.

The bindings that I have spoken of so far were all produced in a slow and laborious manner, as each die had to be impressed separately. Towards the end of the fifteenth century, however, when the printers in England began to issue books of a small size, a new system of binding was introduced, by which the labour of the binder was very considerably lessened, while the amount of decoration applied was increased.

The invention and use of the panel stamp, that is of a large stamp which should ornament the side of the book with one picture, was a great step forward. It was a great advantage commercially as it saved much time, and in some ways it was an advance artistically. By its means the whole side of the book was ornamented at once, instead of by a series of dies impressed one after the other. And as the working out of a binding had ceased to be its main point and the beauty of the die itself was more emphasised, this invention did away with the building up of a pattern altogether, and depended entirely on the excellence in design and workmanship of the stamp. Mr. Weale assigns the date 1367 to the earliest panel stamp known to him, produced by a certain Lambertus de Insula at Louvain, but this is only because the MS. on which it occurs bears that date. Without some further evidence I should be inclined to think this date rather too early, and would not date any panel stamp before the fifteenth century.

There is no doubt that the binders of the Low Countries were the earliest to introduce this style of binding, and they produced very excellent work, and the earliest panel stamps we find in use in England are Netherlandish in execution, either used in this country by foreign workmen, who had come over and settled, or obtained by native binders from abroad. The earliest stamps were no doubt for the most part of metal, and therefore practically indestructible, and we know that they often passed out of the hands of their proper owner and were used by other binders, even though the name of their original owner was engraved upon them. As an example I may mention a book-cover in the Douce collection in the Bodleian, on which two stamps are impressed side by side. One has the name John Guilibert, the other the inscription: " Omnes sancti angeli et archangeli dei, orate pro nobis. Ioris de Gavere me ligavit in Gandavo." A still more marvellous example, and one almost certainly bound in England, is in the Library of Corpus Christi College, Oxford. It has on the two covers, besides innumerable dies, no less than nine panels, two signed Woter Vanduffle, three signed Martinus de Predio, and four signed Jacobus, illuminator. The binding almost looks like a sample put out to show a specimen of every stamp and die in the establishment. The Woter Vanduffle stamp seems very early. I have in my own collection an English heraldic MS. of about the middle of the fifteenth century or slightly earlier in its original binding impressed with the two panels of that binder.

In these earliest panels the inscription nearly always runs perpendicularly, either in the centre of the panel, cutting it in two, or at the side of the picture. One peculiarly distinctive feature of the earliest panels is the presence of four indentations more or less deep and clearly defined at each corner. These were made most probably by the heads of the nails by which the metal plate was affixed to a block before used for stamping. These four marks never seem to occur in later panels, which, if they have any, have only two, considerably larger in size, one at the top and one at the bottom. It has long been a vexed question as to whether these stamps were made of metal or of wood, but it is probable that both materials were used, and that the majority of English stamps were wood. As no heat was applied, and the leather treated when it was damp and soft, a wooden stamp would be sufficiently strong, and I have found by experiment that soft leather takes an excellent impression from a wooden block. I have, however, in my own collection a binding struck from a broken plate, and the appearance of the break shows clearly that the stamp must have been of metal.

The earliest definitely English panel stamp is on a loose binding in Westminster Abbey Library. It has on it the arms of Edward IV., with two small supporting angels. The rest of the binding is covered with small dies, one in the shape of a heart, the other a *fleur de lys*. It is a great pity that the book which was in this binding has been lost, as it might have contained some clue to information about the binding.

Wynkyn de Worde, in spite of his enormous business, does not seem to have ever used a panel with his name or device, at least so far not one has been found, but with other printers and stationers the case is different. Pynson used two panels. One is a copy of one of his devices, having his initials on a shield with the helmet and crest above, while around all is a floral border. The other has in the centre a large Tudor rose, surrounded by intertwined branches of vine leaves and grapes. This latter panel was a popular one, and several variations of it are to be found, all of which are probably of the fifteenth century.

The only copy at present known of the Pynson panel with his mark was acquired not long ago by the British Museum. I had known of the existence of the copy for some time, as it had belonged to a Manchester bookseller who had described it to me. He had sold the book, but had no record of the purchaser, and knew nothing of him further than that he lived in London. One day while I was working in the Museum a visitor came in with this identical book and offered it for sale. The book itself was a copy of the *Abridgement of the Statutes* of 1499. Herbert, in his *Typographical Antiquities*, describes a copy of the *Imitation of Christ*, printed by Pynson, which was in a similar binding, and perhaps that may still be in existence; but I am sorry to say that the collectors of the beginning of the present century ruthlessly destroyed all old bindings, and would not have anything on their shelves except bound in morocco or russia by Roger Payne or Charles Lewis. There is not one single old leather binding in the whole of the Spencer Library, though we know that many of the books when bought were in their original covers.

Frederick Egmont, the stationer about whom I spoke in my last lecture, had several panels. The first has as its central ornament the Tudor rose, and round it are vine leaves and grapes. Round the whole is an arabesque floral border containing the initials and mark of Egmont. This design was common at the time, there being several other panels almost identical, one of which was used by Pynson. Another more important panel is an almost exact copy of the device of Philippe Pigouchet, the Paris printer. A wild man and woman, standing on either side of a tree covered with some kind of fruit, bear in one hand flowering boughs while with the other they assist in supporting a shield suspended by a belt from the branches above them. Upon the shield are Egmont's mark and initials. The device of the wild man and woman was for some reason very popular at this time and for a short period afterwards. It was used by Bumgart at Cologne, and at Edinburgh by Walter Chepman and Thomas Davidson. It was used by Pigouchet and other Parisian printers, and by Peter Treveris, who printed in Southwark at the sign of the "Wodows," and the references to it in colophons are very numerous. This panel of

Egmont's not only bears his mark and initials, but is inscribed on the lower margin, "Fredericus Egmondt me f[ecit]". Three copies only of this binding are known, a very fine copy at Caius, a poor copy at Corpus, and one in my own collection. Books which are stamped on the front with this panel generally have on the back a plainer panel containing three rows of arabesques of foliage surrounded by a border, having ribbons in the upper and lower portion inscribed with the names of the four evangelists. This panel not infrequently occurs alone, without Egmont's signed panel, and may have been left by him in England when he returned to France.

Nicolas Lecomte, the other foreign stationer settled in England in the fifteenth century, and to whom I alluded in my last lecture, also used panels with his initials and mark. He had not a pictorial panel, but a formal one of rather Low Country type. The centre of the panel is divided into two parts, each containing four spirals of foliage encircling the figures of beasts and birds, while around all is a border of grapes and vine leaves. At the bottom of the border are the initials N. C., with a mark which almost exactly corresponds with the initials and mark found in his device in the books printed for him. A very fine specimen of this binding is in the University Library.

The majority of the early panels are pictorial, and in some cases are very elaborate and ornamental. The pair used by a binder whose initials were A. R. are especially fine. On one side is the salutation of Elizabeth with the Almighty and the Holy Ghost above, in the top corners are the Tudor emblems, the rose and portcullis. Round the whole is a diaper border with a shield in each corner, one the arms of St. George, another of the city of London, a third with two cross swords, and a fourth with two cross keys. The panel on the other side has in the centre St. John standing preaching to some people who sit in the foreground. On the left is St. James, on the right King David, while the lower part is taken up with a picture of David and Bathsheba. This binding is very rare, and I know of only two examples, one in my own collection and one in the University Library. This binder had several other panels; there is one in the University Library with a figure of St. Roche, and there are two on a book at Aberdeen with the Baptism of Christ, and the Annunciation.

It is curious that the subjects of these panels should have been invariably religious, scenes from the Bible or pictures of saints, and that we never find subjects from popular stories. The most frequent subject of all was I think the Annunciation, and then single figures of saints, St. Barbara being one of the most popular. The binder very often used a panel with a figure of the saint after whom he was named. Nicolas Spering, who worked at Cambridge, has a panel with the picture of St. Nicholas restoring to life the three children who had been killed and pickled by the innkeeper. Another binding which is probably English, though it might be French, has on one side St. Barbara with her palm branch and three-windowed tower, and on the other the Mass of St. Gregory. In the border there occurs a delightful little figure of a mermaid with a comb in one hand and a looking-glass in the other.

About 1500 a particular pair of panels came into great vogue amongst the bookbinders. One had upon it the arms of England, supported by the dragon and greyhound, the other the Tudor rose supported by angels. Round the rose runs a ribbon with the motto:—

> Haec rosa virtutis de celo missa sereno
> Eternum florens regia sceptra feret.

In the top corners we generally find shields with the arms of St. George and of London, while in the base below the rose or shield occur the initials and marks of the binders. This general use of the royal arms, together with the use of the arms of London, points, I think, to some trade guild to which these binders belonged. Foreigners, though they might still use the royal arms, do not use the city arms, putting something else in the place, sometimes the French shield, sometimes merely an unmeaning ornament. It is a very popular but erroneous opinion held by a great many people that these bindings with the royal arms were produced for the king, Henry VII. or Henry VIII. as the case may be. It would be just as reasonable to imagine that all the shops with the royal arms over the door were private residences of the queen. Of course, the fiction is kept up in order to increase the price of the books; " from the library of Henry VIII." looks well in catalogues. Even in the sumptuous work recently issued on the historic bookbindings in the Royal Library at Windsor this mistake has been repeated.

A very large number of these bindings exist, all very similar, but unfortunately, although in many cases they bear the binder's initials and mark, we cannot discover his name, on the other hand again we know the names of many binders, but we cannot identify their work; the mere fact that the initials on a binding agree with the initials of a binder's name does not of necessity determine that the particular binding was produced by that binder; a good deal more proof is necessary.

A certain number of these bindings have been settled as the work of a certain man in another way. When the binder was a printer, or a stationer of sufficient importance to have books printed for him, then we can identify the mark on his bindings by means of the mark used in the books.

For instance, to take an early example. We have bindings by Julian Notary, the printer, which bear his initials and mark, and the mark, of course, is the same as the one he uses in his books, while in them his name is in full. So again the work of Henry Jacobi, an important London stationer of the early sixteenth century, was traced by the mark which he uses in some of his books.

We know the names of a considerable number of early binders from the registers of the grant of letters of denization, but unfortunately we have no link between them and the bindings. In this country it was not necessary, as it was in some parts of the Low Countries, to register the design of a binding, and though many of the Low Country bindings look the same, you will find on examination that the detail always varies and each design was protected.

The binder who is best known in connexion with these stamped bindings is John Reynes, whose work is by far the most commonly met with, and who is almost the only producer of stamped bindings mentioned by any early bibliographer. His best-known panel is called " Redemptoris mundi arma," and consists of all the emblems of the Passion arranged in a heraldic manner upon a shield. Reynes was certainly employed as a binder by Henry VIII., as we know from early accounts, and so far as I have seen all the copies of the King's *Assertio septem sacramentorum*, which remain in their original binding, were bound by him. It is fortunate that Reynes put his mark and name in one printed book, otherwise we should not have been able to identify him as the binder. He had also two very well-executed panels, one depicting the fight of St. George and the dragon and the other the Baptism of Christ.

The period during which these panel stamps were produced in England was roughly the forty years from 1493 to 1533. The passing of the act against foreign workmen in the latter year had no doubt a good deal to do with the falling off of the work, but the invention of a binding tool called a roll seems to have finally put an end to the use of the panel. The roll was a tool made in the form of a wheel which saved a very great deal of time in ornamenting the sides of a book, and which was used very widely in England during the sixteenth century. At first when the roll was broad and well cut, as the earliest examples almost always were, it produced a very satisfactory appearance, but it soon became narrower and more finely cut, and therefore showing to much less advantage on the side of a large book, and finally about the end of the century its use was almost entirely given up.

Almost the earliest and the finest of the roll bindings were those produced by the Cambridge stationers. Nicholas Spering beside his panel had several fine rolls which contain his initials and mark.

Naturally the foreign booksellers who sent books over to England found it to their advantage to put them into popular bindings, such as would attract purchasers, and many of these bindings have a distinctly English character. The exploits of St. George and St. Michael are favourite subjects, and are often treated in a most decorative manner. There is one specially fine example dating from about 1500, and probably Rouen work, which has St. George on one side and St. Michael on the other. The binder has not put his initials, but his device, which occurs on one side, is a head on a crowned shield. It is worth noticing that the material of which these foreign bindings are made is often sheepskin rather than calf, which is nearly always used in English work. One binder, whose initials were A. H. and who used the Tudor rose, though without the arms of London, produced very good work, but almost always on this sheepskin, which was not a suitable leather for giving a clear impression.

It is very interesting to watch how in the later panel bindings the lettering gradually deteriorated and became simply part of the ornament. I have three panels, all copied one from the other, and in the first the legend running round the panel is quite clear and correct. In the second the letters are confused, though the general appearance of each separate word is preserved and they can be read. In the last example letters and words are all run together, and the general result is wholly unreadable.

So, too, the old style of work with the pictures of saints or biblical scenes was given up about 1530 for bad renaissance patterns of pillars and classical heads, which are so uninteresting, not to say ugly, that we can hardly regret the speedy disuse of the panel stamp.

Now it must always be remembered that in England at any rate very few of these early bindings are signed, and that therefore to assign particular bindings to particular men is not often possible, but comparison may enable us to attribute them to particular districts and even to particular places. What is wanted is that every small point about these bindings should be studied carefully and compared in different examples, because it is mainly by circumstantial evidence that we can arrive at any knowledge about them. We must class our bindings by a system similar to that lately adopted for identifying criminals. The presence or absence of one particular point merely divides a number of bindings into two divisions. This point, taken in conjunction with a second point, narrows the field immensely, and we can soon put the bindings into groups more or less accurately.

Any one who works at all amongst old bindings will soon begin to note points which are common to certain bindings, and which most probably mean a certain thing. For instance, any one working at the subject would soon perceive that as a rule octavo or quarto books in an English binding have three bands to the back, that is three projecting ridges on which the leaves are stitched, while foreign bindings have four or more. Of course this is not an absolute rule, but it will be found correct in nine cases out of ten. To take another local instance. A very great number of early Cambridge bindings, and some that may have been produced at places not far distant, are remarkable for the curious red colour of the leather used. The binding has the appearance of having been painted over with red, and then the red almost all rubbed off again. This is probably caused by some peculiarity in the process of tanning or dressing. Whenever I see this curious red colour I promptly put down the binding as a Cambridge one, and a more careful examination generally proves it to be correct.

If the boards of the binding have a groove running down the edge you may be fairly certain that the book inside is printed in Greek. If a binding has four clasps, one at the top and bottom as well as two in their usual place, you may be sure that the binding is Italian. Most of these old bindings had clasps or ties of ribbon to keep them shut, but in nearly all cases these have disappeared, and the reason is this. In the early times books were always put on the shelves back first and with the fore edge to the front on which was written the title of the book. Naturally, when readers wanted to take down a book they pulled at it by the clasp or ribbon till that came off, just as now-a-days when books are placed backs outwards the ordinary reader pulls them out by the top of the back, till that comes off. In many cases the ribbons were of alternate colours, a white opposite to a green and a green opposite a white. Of course as soon as books were put in the shelves with the backs outwards the use of ribbons was discontinued, for it was awkward to push into its place a book with two large bows of ribbon in front. This use of ribbons you will notice has been lately revived by some faddists who have no sense of the fitness of things.

These bindings that we have been considering were of course what we should call trade bindings or publishers' bindings. Very few people seem to have had books especially bound for them, and those kind of bindings had generally gilded ornaments upon them, which are not found on early stamped work. The custom of impressing coats of arms on books did not begin until about 1535, when it was started by some Scottish collectors, the earliest known armorial stamp having been used by William Stewart, Bishop of Aberdeen.

The books specially bound for Henry VIII. were ornamented in what was called the Venetian manner, that is with tools obtained perhaps from Venice, but clearly cut in imitation of those used by Aldus for his bindings; the binder of these books was the well-known stationer, Thomas Berthelet.

While these bindings and their designs afford valuable bibliographical information, the materials employed in making the bindings are also often of great importance. The boards were often made of refuse printed leaves pasted together, and were always lined, after the binding was completed, with leaves of paper or vellum, printed or manuscript. To show you how important these fragments may be, I may mention that of the books printed in England or for England in the fifteenth century no less than fifty-three are known only from fragments obtained from bindings. The great find of Caxton fragments made by Blades at St. Alban's I have mentioned before. Not long ago I took to pieces the boards of a primer of Edward VI. and obtained the title and some other leaves of Constable's *Epigrams*, printed by Pynson in 1520, and of which but one perfect copy is known, four leaves of a Whitinton's *Grammar* printed by W. de Worde, eight leaves of an early *Abridgement of the Statutes*, probably printed by Middleton, a perfect copy of an unknown edition of the *Ordynaunce made in the time of ye reygne of kygne Henry VI. to be observed in the Kynges Eschequier by the offycers and clerkes of the same for takyng of fees of ye kynges accomptis in the same courts*, printed by Middleton, and last an unknown broadside ballad relating to the burning of Robert Barnes in 1540, printed for Richard Bankes by that little-known printer, John Redman, who put his name only to one or at the most two known books.

From a binding in Westminster Abbey some years ago came two leaves of an unknown early Cambridge book, Lily's *De octo orationis partium constructione*, edited by Erasmus, and lately at Oxford Mr. Proctor found in a binding in New College some fragments of a *Donatus* on vellum, printed by Caxton, a hitherto unknown book. As Bradshaw said over twenty years ago: " It cannot be any matter of wonder that the fragments used for lining the boards of old books should have an interest for those who make a study of the methods and habits of our early printers with a view to the solution of some of many difficulties still remaining unsettled in the history of printing. I have for many years tried to draw the attention of librarians and others to the evidence which may be gleaned from a careful study of these fragments; and if done systematically and intelligently it ceases to be mere antiquarian pottering or aimless waste of time."

Of course the majority of fragments found in bindings are of no value, and should not be moved; indeed, fragments should never be taken out of bindings unless it is absolutely necessary, for by doing so the binding is almost certain to suffer some injury.

To study effectively the early English book a certain knowledge about these early bindings is required, for the printer, as we have seen, was probably his own binder. What I said about the stationers applies also to the binders, their history is an almost unworked subject, new details are found from time to time, but we have no work on the subject to which we can add them, and our knowledge at present consists mostly of isolated facts. Bradshaw, writing twenty years ago, spoke of the subject as still in its infancy, and I am afraid that English bibliographers cannot boast of much progress. This is not, perhaps, to be much wondered at when we consider how few are willing to work on in the steady, quiet way which he practised and taught. We can do no better than follow in the path that he pointed out, add fact to fact, and detail to detail, avoiding vain theories and idle speculations, so that whatever advance we make in our knowledge of the subject, whether it be much or little, it may at any rate be accurate, and serve as a secure foundation for the work of the future.

THE END.

ABERDEEN UNIVERSITY PRESS.

www.ingramcontent.com/pod-product-compliance
Lightning Source LLC
Chambersburg PA
CBHW030906170426
43193CB00009BA/746